# Bruised but Not Broken

## My Life with a Sociopath

## TONI PETERSON

**BALBOA.**
PRESS

A DIVISION OF HAY HOUSE

Balboa Press books may be ordered through booksellers or by contacting:

Balboa Press
A Division of Hay House
1663 Liberty Drive
Bloomington, IN 47403
www.balboapress.com
1 (877) 407-4847

Because of the dynamic nature of the Internet, any web addresses or links contained in
this book may have changed since publication and may no longer be valid. The views
expressed in this work are solely those of the author and do not necessarily reflect the views
of the publisher, and the publisher hereby disclaims any responsibility for them.

The author of this book does not dispense medical advice or prescribe the use of any technique as a form of
treatment for physical, emotional, or medical problems without the advice of a physician, either directly or
indirectly. The intent of the author is only to offer information of a general nature to help you in your quest
for emotional and spiritual well-being. In the event you use any of the information in this book for yourself,
which is your constitutional right, the author and the publisher assume no responsibility for your actions.

Any people depicted in stock imagery provided by Getty Images are models,
and such images are being used for illustrative purposes only.
Certain stock imagery © Getty Images.

ISBN: 978-1-9822-0655-0 (sc)
ISBN: 978-1-9822-0656-7 (e)

Print information available on the last page.

Balboa Press rev. date: 06/13/2018

# CONTENTS

# PROLOGUE

Visiting a psychiatrist is very seldom a pleasant experience. It typically indicates that something has gone wrong in your life. When I tell you that I have visited a number of shrinks in my life, than you obviously know that I have been through some difficult times. I remember one of those occasions quite well.

I had come to know this therapist well and we had worked several years together. The subject that had brought us together was my husband, Frankie, and our difficulties in the marriage. I worked for years to keep our family together, but it was not happening. Frankie was not interested in the marriage, but did spend an inordinate amount of time talking with psychiatrists. Several of them had come to know much about him.

On this particular occasion, the doctor had told me that he was a narcissist and a sociopath. Even though I didn't know how to define those terms, it didn't sound like a good thing.

"What does that mean?" I asked.

She replied, "I know you have heard of Charles Manson?".

"Oh!"

After letting that visual image sink into my mind, I asked, "So what do you do for that?".

Her answer was not encouraging. "Even if he wanted help, which he doesn't, it would take us seven years just to get started."

What she said next was surprising. "You know more about this than we do. We've been studying these conditions almost 40 years and still know very little. You have been living with it everyday for years. People like Frankie never come to us, because they don't think there's anything wrong with them, unless they have already been in jail."

She then asked, "So what are you going to do now?"

I replied, "Honestly, I don't know."
The next words she spoke were the inspiration for this book.
She added, "You need to write a book. You know more about this stuff than we do."
This is the book.

# INTRODUCTION

*Sociopath – A person with a personality disorder manifesting itself in extreme antisocial attitudes and behavior, a lack of empathy, and a lack of conscience for others.*

There are few things better than curling up on the couch, surrounded by pillows or perhaps snuggling with the person you love, for an evening of movie watching. Pop open a beer and grab a bowl of fresh popcorn dripping with sweet butter and you're ready. All you need at that point is a good movie. It's not likely, especially if your movie watching partner is of the opposite sex, you will agree to watch a romantic comedy, so you search for something else. Everyone loves a good story, and crime thrillers are one of the more popular genres among movie buffs, even when we know the identity of the villain.

1Even though you have a good idea about the movie, you can expect a surprise or two. One of the techniques movie makers have used to capture our attention in a good crime drama is to make the villain a sociopath—a person who can't seem to control himself, but can always be counted on to do something horrible and often violent.

These movies and television shows have taught us to believe that a sociopath is usually a mass murderer who feels no sympathy or sorrow for killing. They are portrayed as out of control lunatics with no other recourse but to be violent. It's like they can't help themselves. This notion has been presented to us in such a way that we tend to think that all sociopaths are evil murders. You might be convinced that if you ever met a sociopath, you would know quickly that they are dangerous.

We conjure up a Hannibal Lecter like a character from "Silence of the Lambs." It's someone so out of control and dangerous that he must be chained and locked up for the safety of society. If he is ever set free, then people will die. The term "sociopath" summons up visions of a crazy person, dramatic background music, and a string of dead bodies.

However, that's not exactly true. There are many sociopathic people among us every day. You probably know some of them. It might even be they belong to your family; someone like uncle Fred who frequently yells at his wife for no apparent reason, or perhaps a cousin who always wants to be the life of the party. They might be working in your factory, serving in public office, patrolling the streets in a police car, or tucked away quietly in the house next door. They're not criminals. They might even be likable people and have family and friends who care deeply about them. Like any personality disorder, there are degrees of affliction. The major problem is that there is little hope for improvement or change for someone with this disorder.

It is also interesting that many people who are leading business people have this ailment. We've heard stories of ruthless executives who left a string of abused people on their way to the top. These people have learned to use their disorder to accomplish significant achievements. They are not necessarily physically violent, but the damage they do throughout their life can be devastating.

If you have been around a person without conscience or empathy for other people, you have witnessed, or perhaps even experienced first-hand, the devastation they cause. It is also likely that you have been on the receiving end of their anger and violence. You have certainly been manipulated by their need for something you can provide to them.

I was in a relationship with a sociopath for thirty years. I know firsthand the damage caused and the ruined lives they leave in their wake. It took a long time, but I was finally able to extricate myself from the marriage but to be honest, there is no way to repair the damage caused to my life and my loved ones.

I'm telling my story for a couple of reasons. Foremost, I've had several psychologists over the years tell me that I need to write a book explaining my life with Frankie. As he was in and out of counseling numerous times over the years, the doctors often turned to me to help them understand his traits. There were many things about him that were known only to me, and he was not forthcoming about them, even to the doctors. I think they were convinced that if they were ever going to understand him, they needed to understand me as well.

Secondly, like many people who write a book, I feel it is important to be understood. People have formed opinions about me because of what Frankie has done. That's true, by the way, of anyone who has been with someone for thirty years. We see one another through the lens colored by those who are around us the most.

The most frequent question I have heard over the years is, "Why did you stay married to this guy for so long?"

You will discover as you read my story that I'm not a weak, wimpy battered wife who was afraid to walk away from her abusive person. There were reasons why I stayed, even though I considered, numerous times, shoving him to the curb. It's true, there were times when I thought he was going to kill me, but I cared too much for him to walk away.

Perhaps you might say this is a story about two people trapped in an extremely dysfunctional relationship. I'm certainly not putting all the blame on Frankie. I messed up my share of times, and I'm willing to accept responsibility. I have nothing to hide in telling this story so at times it might seem callous and raw, but it is merely the truth as I have come to understand it after thirty years.

If you choose to judge me after reading my story, that's fine. Frankly, if you do, you'll need to stand in line. The same is true if you want to condemn Frankie. He certainly had issues like all sociopaths, but I think it's important to try and understand what made him tick. There are things I have learned about him in our more than thirty years together that psychologists found interesting.

I've never tried to hide or cover up our flaws, neither Frankie's nor mine. I always told the shrinks that I was an open book and that is the way I'm telling this story. Obviously, since I'm the one telling the story, you will hear it from my viewpoint, so it's not entirely objective. However, it's a story that Frankie would never tell you. He wouldn't even tell the shrinks everything.

If you had the opportunity to sit down and listen to Frankie tell this story, you would probably be mesmerized by his charm. He is a charismatic person and will go out of his way to appear that way to others—especially if he thinks you can do something for him. You will be his friend as long as you have something to offer.

One other thing you would notice initially about Frankie is his appearance. He was a Florida surfer, and he looked the part. He had a surfer's well-built body, complete with an eight-pack, and hair that blew in the breeze. We met in High School when I began dating one of his best friends. I always thought of him as an asshole and he was also a total stoner.

When we married, he weighed about 165 pounds. I remember that because we made a pact that neither of us would gain more than 20 pounds. Other than while I was pregnant, I kept that agreement and continued to be no more than 120 pounds. On the other hand, Frankie is now pushing 300 pounds with a body that is falling apart. Frankie has suffered through countless hours on a psychiatrist's couch and received a variety of diagnoses that all fit his behavior. He has been variously diagnosed with ADHD, multiple personalities (dissociative identity disorder), misogynist, PTSD, bipolar, narcissist, and a sociopath. He also has an addictive personality, especially when it comes to porn, hookers, drugs, and booze. With great practice, he became skilled at lying and blaming others for his problems. You will find accuracy in each of these diagnoses as I describe my thirty years with Frankie.

Over the next few pages, you will learn a great deal about Frankie and me. It has been an adventure because living with a sociopath has very few dull moments. Let me introduce you to Frankie and myself and tell you about my thirty years of living with a sociopath.

# CHAPTER 1

# The Beginning

The blanket beneath me was soft, but I could tell I wasn't on top of a bed. It didn't matter where I was because it felt like I had been asleep for a long time. Even though I should have been rested, there was an uneasiness in my gut, like I had been punched or maybe ate something that didn't belong. I didn't feel the need to jump up and run to the toilet, but my first thought was to go back to sleep and wait until the queasiness passes. Before trying to drift off to sleep again, I decided to open my eyes and see where I was. Once I was able to raise an eyelid, the brightness was unmistakable proof that I was outside. It wasn't cold, but I was definitely outdoors.

It took a few minutes for my eyes to focus and then I realized I was in the front yard of my own house. Actually, I was in the driveway. The hard mattress I felt underneath the soft blanket was concrete. What the fuck? Why am I sleeping in the driveway? Outside? How did this happen? I rolled over on my back and leveraged myself with my right elbow. As I sat up, my eyes surveyed the situation. Yes, this was my house and my driveway. The wood on the front door needed a coat of paint, and the awning hanging over the front porch had an unmistakable swag in the middle. I remember thinking that I needed to get the bushes next to the front steps clipped back because they were blocking the front of the house.

Next to me was my car, parked where I always parked it at night. I knew that car like a mother knows her child's hands. Meticulously, I had replaced, rebuilt, or polished nearly every part of that car. This was undeniably my place.

Nothing was out of the ordinary except for me and the blanket. Oh yes, one other

1

thing—there was a propane heater near my head. It was already late enough in the morning that the thermostat had shut off, and the heating element was cool.

I wasn't sure what had happened or how I ended up sleeping on the driveway, but I needed to get up and get on with things. I hurriedly went into the house, took a quick shower, got dressed and headed off to the shop. Frankie was not around, so I was pretty sure he was at work. I wanted to speak with him to find out what had happened.

The last thing I remembered was being at a concert and drinking a few beers with a couple of new friends. My foot was heavy on the gas as I drove to the shop. I was anxious to talk to Frankie and find out what the hell he had done to me. I had no doubt he was involved.

After you read my story, you'll understand why I was so sure Frankie was responsible for me waking up in the driveway. It's a painful story for me to tell, but it's important that it's told. There are no heroes in this account, only victims who suffered.

My earliest recollections are in Florida. I was probably about Kindergarten age, and I can recall speeding around the driveway in front of our house with one of those *Big Wheels*. You remember them—they were like oversized tricycles made of colored plastic. The goal was to peddle as fast as you can and then turn sharply to make the small vehicle spin sideways like a race car speeding around a dirt track.

The reason this memory sticks with me so clearly is because I was enamored with cars and racing, an interest that I continue to pursue to this day. I'm not sure where that interest came from since I don't know of any auto freaks in my lineage. My dad did love to play "what's that car" on our long winded road trips we did several times a year. I remember watching a movie on television with my Dad, sometime in the 1970's. It was about Shirley Muldowney, and I was fascinated with everything about her. She was a drag racer, the first woman to be an officially licensed driver able to compete in competitions and she actually won a few. That's who I wanted to be a successful woman in the man's world of automobiles.

As you'll discover from my story, I had a great deal of success working with cars as well. She worked with her husband and brought him along with her in her success. I did the same thing. However, there came a point where our similarities disappeared, which perhaps explains why she is who she is and I'm who I am. I was unwilling to fuck the guys at the top in order to get into the boy's game. All the men were married, and I was married, and I was just not willing to go there. Perhaps I could have been equally as famous. I had the cars, the looks, and the ability—just not the willingness to pay that price.

My parents moved from Illinois to Florida in 1972 or 1973, I'm not sure exactly, but it did fit a pattern that I do remember well—Mom liked to move often, kind of like a Gypsy. In fact, it seems like we moved every year and I was always changing schools. First, we moved into an apartment, and a year later they would rent a house. Another year would pass, and they would buy a house. This meant changing schools every year.

I remember one time when Dad didn't like the house they purchased, so we moved back next door to the original house.

The most notable thing about our family life is the horrendous fights between Mom and Dad. I don't mean a little yelling and door slamming. These were fights that would have been worthy of Pay-per-View if you are into that kind of thing. They were knock-down drag-out fights, and either one was capable of coming out on top. My mother was the meaner and more aggressive of the two. To understand the dynamic and impact of these fights, let me explain my parents to you. Dad is the nicest guy you would ever want to meet. He's the kind of guy whenever someone says, "That's the greatest guy in the world," they could be describing my Dad. He was never weak or a pushover, but he always allowed her some space. It took some time before he erupted and joined the fight.

However, Mom was quite different. She had a mouth on her the size of Texas. It's not an exaggeration to say that at times it appeared as if she came straight from hell.

If she didn't get what she wanted she would explode. It was always, without exception, her way or no way.

My father was filthy rich before I was born. I use the phrase "filthy rich" because that's the way it seemed according to the stories I heard. He wasn't wealthy like one of today's billionaires, but they had plenty of money. He worked as a store manager for a large company and then he was promoted to a position where he would travel to a location to set up a new store. He was good at this so he would typically stay for two years, get the store up and running, and then move to another location. The company loved him. That's where he met my mother. She worked for him.

Dad was living quite the life. He was one of the original members of the *Playboy Club* in Chicago. He was single and enjoying life in the big, exciting city. Telling about it later, he explained how the Playboy Bunnies were for sale, which was a good deal for a bachelor with money.

Dad's parents pressured him to get married because they felt he was getting older and they wanted grandkids. Even though he had no interest in marrying, he married my Mom. Once they were wed, Mom quit working. Dad eventually left his job because he wanted a promotion that never happened. He felt like they didn't appreciate him like before and it was time to move on. After that, he worked at a blue-collar job for many years.

Dad and Mom were married when my stepsister, Diane, was four-years-old, which means they had been married for about six years when I came along. By the time I was old enough to realize what was going on, they had a decade of experience in marital fighting. They were good at it.

When Diane's birth father and my mother divorced, they shared custody of my sister. After Mom and Dad married, there was a time when Dad wanted to adopt Diane legally, and they tried to make it happen. He even sat down with her father and attempted to work it out, but he refused. Apparently, he feared losing the right to visit her which is strange because he never tried to stay in contact with her anyway. I might add, coincidently, her father's name is "Dick," and I remember that because we talked about how descriptive his name was of his behavior. His refusal of the adoption was just an ego or a control thing of some kind.

Dad didn't always get upset with Mom's antics, but occasionally his patience wore out, and he would lash back at her. My sister, who was ten years older than me, would often drag me out to the car and drive away when a fight broke out. It was her way of protecting me from the anger and abuse that always occurred when they fought. Although she tried, Diane was not always able to protect me from these skirmishes, and I witnessed far too many.

One of their fights was precipitated by Dad's glasses. For some reason (remember, Mom usually got mad when she wasn't getting something), Mom had taken his glasses and crushed them. He was truly upset about this one and actually plastered her up against the wall.

On another occasion, she started on one of her crazy rants and Dad decided to just get out of the house. Before he could pull out of the driveway, she ran out and stacked bricks on the hood of his car. I'm not sure what she was trying to accomplish with that stunt, but it's an example of how irrational she became when she was angry.

Hanging on a wall in our house were a couple of real swords with a family crest in the middle. During one of their fights, the swords came off the wall, and they went after each other. That was quite a sight—two grown adults staring each other down with swords drawn, ready to inflict a decisive blow. My sister quickly dragged me out of the house for that one, so I didn't get to see the ensuing sword fight, but I noticed later that Dad had a cut on his leg.

When I was six-years-old, my sister moved out the house for the first time. Even though she was just 16 at the time, she was ready to escape the craziness and try to make it on her own. I guess you could say she had limited success because she moved in and out of the house a few times over the next several years. When she ran out of money, she would always come back and stay until she could accumulate enough to move out again.

Although she would never go to a shrink or seek any type of counseling, I'm confident that my mother is Bipolar (manic-depressed in the old days). She was never bad enough to be locked up or put away for a period of time, but her crazy moods were frequent and intense. It wasn't uncommon for her to beat the shit out of us for little or no reason. If she didn't get what she wanted she would take it out on us, even if it had nothing to do with either of us. Since she frequently used my Dad's belt for the beatings, I got smart enough to avoid the worst of the thrashings. When I saw her getting ready to go off, I would go into the bathroom and stuff toilet paper in the seat of my pants to soften the blows. When she yelled, "Go get your father's belt," I would grab it and run. I made her chase me until she was too tired to inflict much damage. I frequently did the exact opposite of what she said just because it was fun and the only way I knew to deal with her anger.

My Mom had what we called a "white glove" technique. When she became angry for some stupid reason, most likely from not getting her way, she would storm into our room and throw everything onto a large pile in the middle of the floor. On her way out the door, she told me to clean it up. When she returned, if everything was not done correctly, she repeated the process.

Like most little girls, I loved playing with *Barbie* dolls. I fussed with their makeup and hair and would get quite creative. Some had rainbow hair or shaved heads. When she got angry, Mom would just rip off their heads and throw them away. She purchased some expensive dolls and placed them in a glass case. Of course, I wasn't allowed to touch them, but when the temptation was just too great for a little girl, I would get a beating.

She and Dad never slept together, and she always stayed on the couch. We were not allowed to make a sound until she woke up or all hell broke loose. She was a night owl, which meant she often slept until noon. I watched cartoons by reading lips. It was special when Dad would get up early and remove us from the house by taking us to the donut shop or out to play somewhere. When it was time to get ready for school, we took care of ourselves. We were not allowed to shower or cleanup because it made too much noise.

According to Diane, our mother was much worse in earlier years. Although she was terrible with me, I do see how she could have been worse, and I recognize a good possibility that over time she became less and less aggressive. I can understand that now, but as a child, the reality is that our home was a hostile place and the only way to survive was to stay out of Mom's path.

All of this is important because it explains why I have never felt safe. Not at anytime or with anyone in my life— I've always lived in fear, or like I had to fight! I went from dealing with the constant fear of my mother to the even greater fear of Frankie. And Frankie and I fought a lot as if we were oil and water. In many ways, they are alike. In fact, one of the reasons it never felt strange being with Frankie is because it was just like being with Mom. She would rant and scream and throw things and he would kick holes in the wall or tear up furniture and appliances.

My Grandma, on my mother's side, was from Tennessee, and she was not against using robust methods of punishment with her kids. Her instrument of choice was a switch from a nearby tree or the cord from her iron. She had it rough, left alone to raise four kids by herself. Most of the time she worked a couple of jobs and the last thing she wanted, or needed, was a house full of screaming, whining kids when she got home. I remember how she would always say, "Don't tell on anybody because if one tells then you're all gettin' it."

Grandma was virtually all alone to raise four kids by herself. I only met my grandfather two times because he was never around. He must have been quite a character, living totally out of touch with the rest of the world. He never registered with Social Security or paid taxes. About the only thing I remember about him is that was in a band where he played a banjo and a guitar. Grandma divorced him when he came one day with his pregnant girlfriend, to the home they shared with their four kids. However, Grandma is not the same personality type as Mom. Grandma was actually a sweet woman. She told me how Mom would yell and scream until she got her way from the first day she was born. Being demanding and fighting for what she wanted was a part of her DNA. My grandmother was not that type of person. She moved the kids out of Tennessee to Illinois when they were still young.

Living in Florida when I was eight-years-old I have a clear memory of being on an airplane with Mom. The next thing I knew is that we were living in Illinois with my grandmother. Nothing was ever explained concerning why or what was happening. Years later I learned from my sister that Mom just left on a whim. No explanation or anything; she simply packed up and left. I guess she finally got fed up with not getting what she needed from Dad and decided it was time for a change. She had only left my dad a note.

In Illinois, my grandmother lived in an apartment above a house owned by my Aunt and Uncle. They had a daughter, my cousin, named Cindy. Mom and I lived with my grandmother. When the adults had to leave for the day, my cousin Cindy was given the task of taking care of me. During that time, we became very close—in fact, she became my best friend and mentor. Wherever she went, I was sure to be there. Cindy was only a few years older than me, and she had complete responsibility for me quite often. She helped shape the person I became.

I was barely more than eight-years-old at the time, and Cindy introduced me to smoking pot. That was a long time ago, and I can honestly say that pot has never been my thing. If you want to sit around eating Cheetos and getting fat that's great, but it's not for me. I'm not interested.

During this time, I also started drinking heavily. Cindy is four or five years older than me, and we both drank a lot. We would have these huge drinking binges where we played a "pass-out" game. What that means is we would cut of air from our throats to make ourselves pass out. It wouldn't surprise me to learn that I have brain damage today from the drinking I did back then. It was wild. As I look back now, it's somewhat surprising that one of us didn't die as a result of the stupid shit we did together.

Dad and Diane were not with us until six months later when they showed up with a giant moving truck. At that point, we moved into a house in Illinois. Diane was there as well, but she was sent to be with her Dad. I'm sure now that the reason she was sent away is because she was heavily into drugs and even had dealers coming to the house. But my drug days had already begun with my cousin Cindy.

Moving out of my grandmother's neighborhood and into a new house didn't slow down my drug usage. In fact, it progressed even further because I met new people at school who introduced me to new stuff. I upgraded. I continued to get drugs from Cindy who was now dealing pills, not just pot.

When I got to Junior High, my drug use snowballed beyond imagination. It was like entering a whirlwind. I met all the right people (for doing drugs, that is). Despite the drugs, I was a good student. So good, in fact, they placed me in the advanced track of classes. But I didn't want to be in the "brainy" classes. I wasn't interested. I flunked myself and returned to the regular classes so that I could skate through without any effort. Besides, I never saw any purpose in learning Latin and other shit I would never use. It was a dumb waste of time which could be better spent partying.

Mom was unhappy with the house they purchased, so they sold it and moved into a duplex. I don't remember much about the place because, with the drugs and my lifestyle, I was seldom home. At one point, my parents split up, and Dad moved to Minnesota. Mom returned to bar hopping and spreading her legs once again for every interesting guy who came along. I don't know if that's why they split up. All Dad did was drink. He had his favorite places. We knew exactly where to find him when he didn't come home, and he would slip me a few bucks and say, "Don't tell your Mom."

At school, one of the problems I encountered was not always fitting in because I was white. Consequently, I had to learn how to fight, both boys and girls. I had a lot of male friends because I liked sports, so I learned to be tough even though I was small. Once when I was only twelve-years-old, I was trapped in a laundry room by three tall black dudes who were friends of mine. All of us frequently played football together. Their goal was to slap me until I cried. They worked for a good thirty minutes, but I never broke down and cried. The one watching the door was a good friend, and he finally talked them into leaving me alone. They eventually just walked away and let me go.

Making it to High School didn't change much. I continued my pattern of skipping classes nearly every day. A couple of weeks into my first year, a football player was stabbed and killed. This was a traumatic experience for the whole school and a reminder of the world we all faced every day. During that time, I was threatened by a gang, so I began carrying a knife with me all the time.

Since I was into drugs and alcohol, I was labeled a problem child. The school didn't know what to do with me, and my home life was in no condition to be of any help. There was no place I could go to get away from the shit in my life. I'm sure that's one of the main reasons drugs and alcohol were so attractive to me. I hated the Chicago area and the schools and my life. All I wanted to do was party, so I just skated through school. We were all unhappy, and home was not a good place to be.

During that time, I'm not sure what Diane was doing. She certainly wasn't around much. I know she was still heavily into dealing drugs. She lived with cousins, friends, and other places just to get by. She finished college during that time because she had a Bachelor's Degree. Later she was making good money and helped Dad land a job.

His leaving certainly didn't make things any better at home. In fact, things became worse if that's even believable. Without him around, it didn't take long to grow weary of Mom's bullshit. We went around and around. When I didn't do what she wanted, she would threaten to beat me and scream that she wouldn't tolerate it anymore. At this point, I was getting too big for her to handle and I didn't care anyway. She didn't scare me now because all she could do was scream and yell. I had been listening to that all my life, so it didn't make any difference.

After a time, she called my Dad to come back home because she couldn't handle me, but he didn't want to be there. He would refer to her as "Mrs. Black or Mrs. White" coming from the 50's movie called the three faces of Eve. In the movie Eve had multiple personalities. Things were snowballing quickly, and something had to be done, or we weren't all going to survive. Dad didn't want to be in the house with her, and I was tired of her as well—nobody wanted to be in the house with her. I was skipping school on most days, and even though I was still young, I knew I needed to get out.

I decided to go back to Florida. I wasn't sure how that was going to work out, but it could only be better than the hell hole I was living in at the time. I told Dad my plans. He thought it over and then announced he was going with me to Florida. We were going back together. It sounded like a great idea to me. Over the years I have given a great deal of thought about why Dad put up with Mom's shit for so long. I have come to the only conclusion that makes sense—he loved her. I don't understand why or how, but he really did. And that's what he always said.

I have also realized there are many similarities between my Dad and me which will become evident as I tell my story. Very early in my life, the differences in my parents became obvious, and I remember making a conscious choice to be like Dad and not Mom. Like him, I'm a sensitive person and I live through my feelings. I'll admit I do have an evil side that comes out far too often, but the reason is because I've been hurt to the point of where I have nothing left. When I see Frankie's foot go smashing through the wall and the crazed look on his face, I get the fuck out of Dodge, or I prepare to stand and fight. That's why I get drunk. It's a way of hanging on, of trying to get through the fight and stay alive.

Like the drunk that survives the car crash.

# CHAPTER 2

# Frankie's Early Life

If you want to appreciate the Grand Canyon and all its beautiful scenery fully, you need to know something about the Colorado River which was instrumental in molding and shaping the rocks and mountains. If you want to know everything about the myriad of species in the rain forest, it's imperative to study the climate and weather conditions that make things thrive and grow the way they do. The same is true with people.

In order to understand another person, you must know something about the people around them and the ones who were most influential in their life. I had a marriage partner, someone I was with for nearly thirty years, so before you can understand my story, I need to introduce you to him. His name is Frankie. When you are with someone that long, not only do you get to know one another but also your life is shaped in many ways by that other person. I am who I am, not only because of genetics and my parents but also because of my marriage. The similarities between Frankie and my Mom are striking. Since I am much more like my Dad, the relationship between Frankie and I mirrored my parent's relationship in many ways.

Learning about Frankie's childhood was a complicated chore because he didn't want to talk about it much. It took years of piecing together bits of information, off the cuff comments, and endless questioning to learn about his past. As I discovered, one of the reasons he didn't talk much about his family is because he didn't know much about them. What I do know about his life and history is pieced together from clues he left over the years and talking with his family members. It was like a spy compiling a report.

When he was young, Frankie's mother moved his Grandfather into their house in order to take care of the old man. However, for most of the time, Frankie was the only one at home, so the predominate caretaking fell upon him. Grandpa needed constant care, complicated by an addiction to porn and booze. Nearly every day he phoned in an order to the neighborhood liquor store and Frankie would walk down the street and pick it up. He would never talk about it, but I suspect Frankie was molested by his Grandfather in some way. It's hard to imagine that a man who had to have fresh porn everyday could keep from sexually harming a young boy who was frequently with him.

Their family was poor, and they lived in such a manner that the neighbors joined together and filed a complaint with the city about the trash around their house. They were given a citation to clean up the yard, or the city would come and do it for them and then send a bill. For two consecutive years, the holiday donations taken up by neighborhood schools found their way to Frankie's doorstep as they were considered the most impoverished people around. He made a joke a few times about him and his siblings having tuna on toast. Another comment was made about their bunnies disappearing from the backyard, but they ate a lot of chicken. He spent time with babysitters, at friends' homes, but was a "latch key" kid all of his early years.

One thing I do know for sure and it didn't require a great deal of research to learn is that his mother was a real bitch. She had a well-earned reputation for frequenting local bars and picking up men for the evening. She divorced her husband when Frankie was born, so he never really had a relationship with his Dad except for weekends. She remarried two more times but none lasted even a year. It was evident that he had a close relationship with his mother, but the way he treated his stepfather was terrible. I tried to encourage him to spend more time with him and to treat him better, but he kept insisting, "I know that's not my real dad. There's something wrong with the way he treats me."

Although his mother had never said anything about him being a stepfather, Frankie noticed something wasn't right. Occasionally, we would joke about Frankie being black because of some of his physical features and looks. One day after Frankie was a grown man while chatting with his mother and her boyfriend, he blurted out, "Am I the milkman's kid or what?"

It was a sudden, startling question—an outburst suggesting something was burning deep within. It seems that everyone in the family except for Frankie and his siblings knew the truth. His mother confirmed his suspicions that he did have a different father, but she provided no specific information other than the man's name. It was quite a shock for Frankie and left him confused and perplexed.

This was an important matter for Frankie. It was obvious that he needed to know something about his back- ground and where he came from, so I hired a private investigator. The investigator dug into his background information and learned that Frankie's birth father had blown his brains out the same month that Frankie and I were married—isn't that the ultimate coincidence. How- ever, he also discovered the names of two of his father's relatives who were living in Missouri. This opened an entirely new avenue of discovery for us as we reached out to them and learned a great deal about his real family on his father's side.

The story that we learned through this process is that prior to Frankie's birth, his mother was working for a large multi-national corporation in the 1960's and his birth father was a big wig with the same company. As you might imagine if you knew Frankie's mother, she screwed the boss and got pregnant. She wanted to keep the baby even though her husband at the time was not the father. Apparently, she and her boss, Frankie's father, only dated three times, and he even offered to marry her, but she declined the offer.

Before the baby was born, he moved to Minneapolis where he stayed for two years. When he returned, he would not even speak with Frankie's mother. Just six months after Frankie was born his mother divorced her husband and claimed that he, the divorced husband, was Frankie's real father. Rather than insisting Frankie's birth father take care of expenses, she pushed it off on her ex-husband, in spite of the fact his birth father was a wealthy man.

This is perhaps the earliest example of the stupid decision-making that characterized Frankie's family life. Whenever she faced an opportunity, she always seemed to choose the option that would cause the most pain and grief. One of the reasons Frankie lived in such poverty is because of these conscious fucked up decisions made by his mother.

The private investigator had identified the relatives living in Missouri, so Frankie flew out there in 1996 to meet his Grandmother and Aunt, the only two living relatives from his father's side of the family. They affirmed that they already knew about Frankie but had no idea where he was or how to contact him. Meeting these two women was the beginning of a remarkable adventure that took us through a variety of twists and turns for the next few years.

His Grandmother was a strict Mormon. Her entire family, except for her husband, came to this country from Denmark and for some unknown reason ended up in Missouri. I don't know if she was a Mormon before arriving in the States or if she converted later, but it was extremely important to her. When he arrived, she insisted that Frankie stay at her house rather than a hotel. She gave him a book that was definitely written by his father, but it was totally insane, making no sense.

A few days after Frankie returned home, he received a letter from his Grandmother saying that she was entirely disowning him. She clarified that she didn't like his long hair, his fingernails were dirty, and he dressed like a biker. I guess she couldn't get past her strict religious beliefs about lifestyle, even for the sake of her long-lost grandson. It was a traumatic experience for Frankie. He had never been on an airplane, so he was scared both coming and going. He was introduced to two crazy old ladies, speaking mostly in Danish, and because he didn't live or act like a Mormon, they wanted nothing to do with him. We both tried to reach out to the Grandmother, but she wouldn't talk to either of us.

That incident changed him in many ways—how he felt about his mother, his father, about everything because all that he thought he knew up to that point had been a lie. Not only was he an angry guy to start with, but this made it much worse. As you will discover in the pages of this book, his Aunt appears in the story again. Even looking back over every aspect of our relationship with these women in Missouri I find very little that was positive about meeting them. It's probably accurate to say that our life would have been better, at that time, if Frankie had never learned about his father and family.

As early as Kindergarten, Frankie's mother took him to a psychologist, and he was diagnosed with ADHD. The doctor put him on Ritalin which probably wasn't a good idea, but they were trying to deal with Frankie's rage. It seems he had been angry from the day he was born. At about age 12 or 13, he began to have suicidal thoughts. During that time, he met an older guy who lived down the street, and he hung out with a bunch of other guys. The man and his friends were dealing drugs. Frankie liked the new stuff better, so he dumped all his Ritalin down the toilet and started doing street drugs.

The bunch of them went off on camping trips in the woods several times. I don't know for sure, but I've always wondered if perhaps Frankie was sexually molested on some of those trips. He has a lot of issues with sex that must be rooted in something he experienced early in his life. He has also been labeled by the shrinks as a misogynist, as a man who hates women. I'm not sure if he hates women or if he just sees them solely for the purpose of his pleasure and well-being. I don't know if it was molestation or his addiction to porn, but his whole attitude toward sex was totally messed up.

I've always felt sorry for Frankie because he had a shitty life, from the outset. I don't think he has ever experienced what it means to be loved by anyone. His first breaths were in the context of a family filled with lies and craziness. He has been lied to by others constantly— that's all he knows. Consequently, he's incapable of loving himself. Perhaps the most amazing thing is that he's not in worse condition than he actually is, which is pretty ugly. The Missouri trip where he was introduced to his father's side of the family was kind of like the straw that broke the camel's back. It was terrible to discover a new family and then find out they were worse than the lousy family he already had.

One of the big blows from this new information was learning that his birth father lived less than ten minutes away from him his whole life. We never discovered if his birth father was aware of that situation. His Missouri relatives claimed they had no idea where Frankie lived. From the moment he became aware that he had a father he had never met, Frankie had a longing to meet the man and learn his side of the story. When he found out that he was just minutes away the entire time, it was devastating. It was obvious he had no interest in contacting his own son. His mother said the only thing Frankie's Dad ever gave her was some books of *Green Stamps* that she used to purchase a baby stroller.

His father, who worked for a huge corporation, was heavily involved in a legal case concerning charges that the company was operating as a monopoly. It was a major case in the 1980's in the Federal Court system. He secretly taped meetings that he had been involved with and we were told that he used the tapes to blackmail company officials. Of course, he was fired, and they also had him committed to a mental facility twice. He was a severe drug and alcohol addict, a typical product of the 60's hippie culture. He was diagnosed a narcissist and a sociopath. The majority of photos we had of him, he was either naked or wearing very little clothing. He also kept multiple girlfriends and was probably a sex addict as well.

He made an unusual pact with himself. He was so vain that he didn't want to live past the age of 50, primarily because he didn't want to get old and look bad. Obviously, he had no sense of the value of human life. It's interesting that Frankie made similar statements about his life as well, although it's apparent his commitment to not looking so bad is not as strong. As I write these words, Frankie's weight has ballooned up over 300 pounds.

Frankie's father tried to commit suicide several times, and each time he made an audio recording and send it to his mother. Everyone in the family thought it was a joke, so they didn't take it seriously enough to do anything to keep it from happening. Eventually, he hired someone to help him and ended up taking a bullet through the mouth. We were never sure if he really did it himself, but it is listed in police records as a suicide.

In 2000, Frankie's grandmother in Missouri died. His aunt, the one who lived with her, tracked us down in Colorado where we were living at the time and called us to break the news. She spoke with Frankie, and they began to look beyond their differences and made a connection. She said she wanted to meet with Frankie, but I resisted and told her I didn't think it was a good idea. I wasn't sure what she wanted or if she was sincere about wanting a relationship. Frankie had been hurt so much that I wanted to be careful.

We eventually made the trip to Missouri without notice and popped in on her unexpectedly. It was unexpected for her but entirely intentional for us. By catching her off guard, I hoped it would be easier to discern her intentions. In spite of the surprise, she was amazingly nice. In fact, I would say that she turned out to be one of the finest people I've ever known. Over the next couple of years, it was obvious that she had some quirky ideas, but she was always extremely nice to all of us.

She filled us in on a great deal of the family history, providing information we would never have known from any other source. Apparently, in Denmark, Frankie's Grandmother was considered royalty, and her family even owned a castle. She was suicidal and considered a "handful", I was told. However, the love of her life was a peasant whom she was forbidden from seeing. She had cheated on her husband and produced his father just like Frankie's story. History repeating itself as his father learned of this at age 30 also. We were told they didn't know the exact name of his fathers' family lineage, but I always thought they knew but just didn't want to tell us. Either way, we have no idea the real name of his birth father.

Before completing the description of Frankie's family, I need to add that his mother is also a drug addict. In fact, she possesses many of the same issues that plague Frankie. She is probably Bipolar, as well as his sister who was diagnosed and they only share the mothers' dna. She's been on Prozac since the day it was invented. Her mental abilities spiraled down quickly after Frankie was born, and they continued to get worse from then on. She takes a massive cocktail of pills in addition to Prozac, and recently the more heavy duty pills for mental issues.

The legacy Frankie received from his family was mental illness and parents on both sides with fucked up families. It was essential to learn these things because it helps me better understand Frankie and the problems we had together. It's hard for people to break a cycle of addiction and mental illness as it's often passed from one generation to the next, both by nature and by nurture. That also points to another reason for my interest in understanding Frankie. He is the father of my children, and I see some of the same qualities in them. My quest to understand Frankie has been motivated by my desire to understand better and help my children.

When you understand our histories and temperaments, it's not surprising that Frankie and I lasted so long together. We were just living out what we had been taught all our lives. Neither my family nor his family was able to break the cycle of violence, addiction, anger, and dysfunction, so the question became, can one of us change the pattern? In the end, I finally realized it could not be changed. I have also realized that you can't help people who don't want help. It's impossible.

I'm confident that there are not many people who would have lasted a few short years with Frankie, much less the three decades I endured. How was it possible? That's what this book is about. It has been a long and often painful journey, and I want to share it with the hopes that better understanding will lead to better relationships.

# CHAPTER 3

# Getting Together with Frankie

Leaving Mom in Chicago, Dad and I moved back to Florida in the hopes of finding a better situation. I was tired of being physically and verbally abused, and ready to leave the shitty situation at school behind. Dad was also prepared to walk away from all the shit, so when he got to Florida, they were divorced in a rather amicable arrangement. Although I was aware that I was still toting a lot of my own personal issues, I felt a tinge of excitement about the possibility of starting over in a place where I was not already defined by the expectations of others.

Living with my Dad, I began the task of establishing myself in a new place with new people. Even though my attendance record in school while living in Illinois was sketchy, their schools were significantly advanced in comparison to what was going on in Florida at the time. Although I had deliberately tanked the opportunity of being in advanced classes in Illinois, I was still academically far ahead of my contemporaries in the Florida system.

School in Florida was not much better for me. I did attend more often because I wanted to get to know some people and make friends. I was starting from scratch. Every class I walked into was a room of complete strangers, but I was determined to make it work. Plus, going to school was the best way to find parties and drugs, two things that were of great interest to me.

In my second year of high school, I was pulled into the Principal's office to defend myself against all the time missed skipping school. By this time, I had been in and out of trouble a few times already, so I was no stranger to the Principal's office. I went to his office, and we had a good heart-to-heart talk. He wrapped up the discussion by explaining to me that I was advanced enough with my education that there was no point in doing high school any longer. If I was interested, he suggested I take the Florida exit exam, and I could skip the last few years of school. Obviously, I was interested, and I passed with a score of 97%. I did it with only an eighth- grade education from Illinois.

At school, I met a boy named Nick. It turned out that he lived across the street from us, and we walked home together often. During our conversations, I discovered that Nick smoked weed, so we started talking about drugs. Nick was a typical surfer-looking guy with blond hair and blue eyes. Nick and I dated for a while, and during that time I met his friend Frankie. I never once thought about tossing Nick aside to go after Frankie—he just wasn't appealing to me.

Several times, while I was still dating Nick, Frankie would hit on me. His advances didn't go anywhere because I was never attracted to Frankie. I always thought he was an asshole who was just always around because Nick was his best friend. The drugs were why he seemed to hang around. I never thought he was cute at all, so I never gave dating him a second thought. The one thing about Frankie that did catch my attention was that he was the primary drug dealer at his school. He even had some of the staff at the school as customers. That's why we kept in contact.

At one point I discovered I was pregnant with Nick's child. It was certainly not intentional, but it often happens when young teenagers who don't have much sense, get too intimate. During that time, I had constant bladder infections, and I learned, too late, that the bladder medicine canceled out the birth-control pill. By the time I discovered I was pregnant, Nick and I had broken up. In my thinking, getting rid of the child was a no-brainer. I was doing a significant amount of drugs and afraid the child would have severe congenital disabilities. Also, I was way too young to raise a child. It wasn't an easy decision, but I did have an abortion.

I began working at various jobs at 15 with a full-time permit for poverty while I was still in school. Working continued, of course, after I quit school. It has never been difficult for me to find a job, but at the time I was so young that securing a job that paid anything worthwhile was nearly impossible. Typically, I went from one job to another, trying to make more money with each change. When I was not at work, I partied.

During that time, Dad had an automobile accident and lost his eye. Then got a DUI which motivated him to get sober. After the divorce when he and I first moved to Florida, he stayed drunk all the time, and he decided it was time for a change. Once he took that step, I decided to follow his lead. I locked myself in the apartment for six months and got sober. At the time, I was highly addicted to cocaine, but I took other drugs that were available. It was difficult, but I was successful and got rid of the drugs for good.

That was years ago, and I've never gone back to drugs. The only thing I didn't eliminate was alcohol.

Once I was free from the drug usage, I started to go out again with my friends. This time it included Frankie and Jack. Nick, Frankie and Jack were the "Three Muskateers."

During that time, I found myself at a couple of parties with Frankie. Occasionally, I would call Frankie, and he would come over, and we visited. One day, after asking my Dad's permission, he brought a kitten and gave it to me.

Just before he graduated from high school, Frankie learned that his mother was leaving to go live with his grandmother. This meant he had a find a place to live since she basically kicked him to the curb. He rented a room from the parents of his friend Erin and stayed with them for a short time.

Frankie and I had been friends for a year and a half, and one night he asked if I wanted to go to a movie. We went to the neighborhood drive-in, and one thing led to another, and next thing you know, we were dating regularly. It was certainly never a plan, at least not for me—it just happened.

Shortly after we started dating, Frankie and Erin got in trouble, and Erin's parents were really pissed. Frankie, Erin, and another guy across the street were into the heavy drugs now. It was obvious to them that Frankie was part of the problem, so they kicked him out of the house which meant he was entirely out on his own. My sister liked Frankie, and after all, we desperately needed money. She talked to Dad and convinced him to let Frankie move in with us. She sold him on the idea that he could help with food and rent because we were barely making the bills. He was there frequently anyway, so it really didn't make much difference. I was about sixteen at the time.

Even though I quit using drugs, I didn't change my friends and that naturally created problems. Frankie was living with Dad and me, and our incomes were the minimum wage from whatever shit job we could find. While Frankie was living with us, he lost his car and driver's license. His truck was stolen two times. He lost his license for not having insurance when he got into an accident. In order to get around town, he rode a bicycle. I also noticed that frequently, when he came home from school, he smelled like perfume and had lipstick smears on his clothes. When I asked about it, he lied. This was not the first time I had caught him cheating. It was my first introduction to his relentless ability to lie about everything.

I pursued the matter, and we had a huge argument. Finally, he slammed me up against the wall. When I gathered myself, I kicked him out of the house. He collected his stuff, and I waited in the driveway with his bike. When he came out, I rammed him in the balls with his own bike. It was a vicious fight, but he did finally admit that he was seeing other girls.

After Frankie moved out, I discovered I was pregnant again. Like before, I was on birth control along with other medicine. Honestly, however, I didn't think he could get me pregnant. When I told Frankie, he wanted me to have an abortion. When we first talked about it, I sort of agreed and even went to a clinic to do so. It certainly made sense on several levels. We were barely making it financially, and the cost of a child would make things even worse. Also, neither Frankie nor I were no longer together. However, as I was filling out the paperwork, I began to give it more thought. I laid the clipboard down and walked out. I decided that I'm not going to do this again. Instead, I'm taking responsibility.

Months later I gave birth to a little girl, and I named her Catherine. At the time, Frankie and I were not together. In fact, I had been dating another guy, a man I had met at the DMV, a thirty-five-year-old man, Jerry, who was fantastic and took good care of me. My belly got so big that I couldn't even drive, so when I needed to visit the doctor, I called Nick, who lived across the street, for a ride. He was always there for me when I needed him.

I'm not sure if it's true, but I was told before my daughter was born, Nick told Frankie to step away because he was going to take care of the baby. I don't know if it was guilt over giving up the first baby or what he was thinking. After Catherine was born, Frankie's mom showed up at the house one day to see her. Frankie appeared two days later and explained that he had been in a relationship with an ex girlfriend his Mom had set him up with, and he was going to marry. However, when she heard about the baby, she took off. As we were talking that day, I told him that I had listed him with the state as the father and that he would have to pay child support and provide medical insurance.

I warned him that if he didn't want to be in the kid's life to just move on. After all, Nick and Jerry were both fantastic to me. However, if he did want a relationship, then maybe we should get married. He replied that's what he wanted to do, so Frankie and I became husband and wife. I knew at the time it was not my best choice, but I felt I owed it to my daughter and Frankie to give him another chance.

As I review my life today, I confess it wasn't the first bad decision I ever made. However, it might have been the worst. Frankie and I being together was like oil and water—it just doesn't work. Both of us brought a great deal of negative baggage into the relationship in addition to his sociopathology. Perhaps the most amazing thing is that we stayed together for nearly 30 years. I gave it my best shot.

# CHAPTER 4

# A Rough Start to Marriage

My daughter, Catherine, was born on December first of 1987. Since we were primarily living on the edge of poverty, I was dependent on state assistance for medical needs. I understand what it means to say, "beggars can't be choosers," because I went to whatever doctor they offered, and choices were limited.

I'm an independent person by nature, so it's difficult for me to rely on others to meet my needs. Also, this pregnancy was a new thing for me, and I was traveling through uncharted waters. I didn't have a mother available or an experienced woman in my life to provide guidance and encouragement. If you combine that with the natural emotions that accompany hormone changes, it was a difficult time for me.

Both of my pregnancies lasted nearly ten months, and I was growing quite restless, especially with the first. I gained an enormous amount of weight, 50 pounds with each pregnancy, and didn't handle it well because I've always been quite small. The doctor finally decided I had gone far enough and scheduled a time when she would induce labor.

Plans were made, and my mother flew out to Florida from Chicago to be there for the birth of her first grand- child. We traveled the short distance to the hospital for an early morning check-in. We were eager and anxious at the same time. Once I was situated and the medicine administrated, the only thing to do was wait. And we did. In fact, we waited all-day long.

Even with the medicine to speed things along, labor was not moving rapidly, in fact, it seemed like it was going nowhere. At about 11:30 that night, a new doctor came in to check on my progress. I had been there since 7:00 that morning, given two epidurals and an enema. I was tired, discouraged, and ready for something to happen. The new doctor examined the situation and declared that if I'm not dilated to a certain point shortly, then he was going to do a C-section. He made it clear that he was ready to get finished and get home.

I have never liked being treated as an object and had no interest in hearing him gripe about wanting to go home. I'm the one who had been there struggling all day long. He simply showed up ready to do something. He was nothing more than an annoying ass.

I told him, 'I don't give a shit if you want to go home!"

A doctor should have known better than to treat a woman in my condition that way.

I ordered the nurses to unplug everything and then told the doctor I would see him in an hour. I'm not sure what I planned on doing, but whatever it was, it worked. Within an hour I was in the delivery room. Catherine was born without any problems. Everything went well after all the waiting and anticipation, and the baby was perfectly healthy. After the delivery, I only stayed a day and a half in the hospital.

Once Catherine and I were at home, it was time to examine our current situation and make plans for what was going to be our future. Frankie had made it clear that he wanted to be the father, but I wasn't at the point of putting my trust in him altogether. I knew how unpredictable and unstable he was and even though I was still young myself, I knew that it would be difficult to build a stable family with him. I will say, not once during our marriage did I bring up the past about him leaving while I was pregnant.

I decided to give Frankie some time to see if he was serious about wanting to be a father and provider. It wasn't like I set up a series of tests or asked him to jump through a bunch of hoops; I just wanted to see how he handled the new baby and additional responsibility. Frankie had secured a full-time job working for a former next-door neighbor, Dan. He owned a company that did demolition work. In addition to working, he had completed school at night to learn graphic design which he never used. I observed for two months, and it was February (1988) before we finally took the marriage vows. I was still somewhat hesitant about trusting Frankie entirely, but I felt it was important for Catherine to have a father in her life. I knew how important my father was to me and how difficult my life was when he wasn't around. I didn't want that for her.

A wedding is typically an extravaganza, especially for a young bride and her first marriage. Our wedding was kind of a joke. There was no wedding chapel with fancy decorations and an expensive reception. Money was in short supply and finding a way to pay for a wedding was of no interest to either of us. We were both trying to figure out how to be parents and manage life with a new baby. We were both very young and knew little about life and how to have a regular marriage and family. Neither of us had experienced anything close to a loving home life with caring parents.

We had our wedding at the beach. Since Frankie was big into surfing, the beach was like a second home for us. In addition, back in those days, having a wedding on the sand was free, which made it a perfect fit for our budget. We had somewhat of a thrown together reception in a friend's backyard, not unlike numerous other parties we had with friends on a regular basis. For our honeymoon, we spent the day at a local amusement park. Frankie's Mom paid for us to stay in a shitty hotel nearby and we topped off the whole event with both of us getting crabs. Not romantic in any way.

Before Frankie and I started dating, I had completely stopped doing drugs. However, Frankie was still using and selling large quantities of weed, so that meant there was a steady stream of traffic in and out of our house. I was afraid this was a huge red flag for neighbors that something unsavory was happening at our place. I was willing to accept Frankie having pot around the house and selling it to his friends, but I was not interested in having the police stop by and hauling him off to jail, or my kids for the fact that it was illegal. I was still not sure he was even going to stick around and live up to his family responsibilities, and a trip to jail would have ended that for sure.

In order to keep nosey neighbors from calling the cops, I created a diversion. I purchased a pool table and set it prominently in the garage, where I insisted all the drugs and dealings must stay away from family, and kept the door raised most of the time. There was nothing suspicious about having a pool table in the garage. Frankie and his friends (customers) could transact their business around the pool table, and from across the street, it looked like they were having a friendly game of pool. I also installed a kegerator in the garage later on, not so much for Frankie and his friends, but for me. Although I was not doing drugs any longer, I still drank beer and always had it nearby.

Frankie had another addiction that reared its ugly head during the early months of our marriage—porn. I knew when we were dating, but didn't understand or know how bad it was, as our sex life was great! I'm not a prude by any stretch of the imagination, and I certainly understand that men like to look at naked women. I don't have a problem with that, but that's not what I'm talking about. Frankie was addicted to the stuff. This seemed to get worse as the time went by.

He spent far more time studying those magazines than he did with me and that's something I've never understood. It's not like I'm homely or have a pudgy, misshapen body, or some other grotesque feature that's repulsive to look at. I'm a good-looking woman. I would even go so far to say that I'm sexy and hot. I'm short, my weight is appropriate and as I said earlier has remained the same since Frankie and I first met.

I'm not crazy about doing kinky stuff, but I'm willing to try. If he ever wanted me to perform a particular way in the bedroom, except trading or adding partners, I was always up for the challenge. Things had escalated when my son was born. He even gave some of his magazines to an 11 year old boy down the street who became addicted. Later on, he would introduce this same guy to the meth dealer in the neighborhood, and he's addicted to that as well. I didn't push him away nor did I ever withhold sex from him, yet he was still addicted to porn. Somehow, he found more there than just sex. Like any addiction, it got a grip on him, and he couldn't escape.

Not only did I have to deal with Frankie's addictions to drugs and porn, but he also had a propensity for violence. During our 30 years of being together, I was on the receiving end of his violent rage more than once. However, one of the first experiences came early in our relationship when we were out playing mini-golf one evening. The game of golf can be frustrating and rage inducing, and we've all seen images and videos of golfers throwing clubs into the water or wrapping them around a tree.

But we weren't playing golf—it was mini-golf, the kind where you put the ball through a clown's mouth, into a windmill, around a few obstacles, and into the hole. It's the kind of game you play when you want a relaxing evening outdoors. If you make a good shot and the ball goes into the hole, everyone laughs and enjoys the moment. If you miss a shot, your friends might sneer or joke, but it's all good-natured fun.

Not for Frankie. During the course of our game, he went on a massive rant. For the first few seconds, it was kind of funny as he grabbed several golf balls and heaved them as far as he could and he even tossed a couple of golf clubs into the night. It didn't take long to realize he was not just blowing off a little steam. He started screaming and cussing at everyone who was within earshot. People were backing away from us, and everyone was a bit afraid of what he might do next. It was quite a sight as mothers and fathers dragged their kids away and everyone who stayed just stared, not knowing what to do next.

It was a terribly embarrassing scene, and I ended up walking home by myself. I wasn't worried about Frankie. I didn't even expect to see him at home later that night because I was sure he was going to jail as soon as someone called the cops. I didn't want to be a part of that mess and wherever it might lead. It was one of the early lessons I learned about Frankie—you have to be willing and able to walk away from a fight, especially if it's not something vital for you.

Apparently, no one called the cops, or perhaps he left the scene before they arrived, but Frankie showed up at home that evening as if nothing had happened.

Frankie, Catherine, and I continued to live with Dad after we married, but that didn't last long. We wanted a place of our own, so we moved out. I was hopeful we would do better with a fresh start. However, that was a short-lived adventure as well, primarily because of financial reasons. We were in a situation where none of us was making much money, and we needed to pool it together for all of us to survive. When we moved out, Dad invited my friend Nick to move in as his roommate and help with expenses, but that wasn't working out for him either. I searched for a place for all of us and three months later found a house, and we all moved back in together. My dad was spending all his time off with Catherine already helping me with babysitting.

It only took a short time for all of us to settle back in together. Once everything was comfortable and everything going smoothly, I decided it was time for another baby. Catherine was two years old, and I felt she needed a playmate. She had almost grown out of her colic stage. It didn't take long before I was pregnant.

I would like to say that the thought of a second child helped Frankie calm down, but it didn't. His violent tendencies made another appearance one day when Catherine was having a fit—typical for a two-year old with colic. I sat her down to talk and get her back on track. Frankie swooped in, grabbed her up, and slapped me across the face. I was pissed, to say the least.

I knew I had to get away before one of us was seriously injured, so I ran out the front door and climbed into my car. Frankie, in an attempt to stop me from going anywhere, ran out onto the driveway. As I backed out of the driveway, I tried to hit him with the car—honestly, I had hoped to hit him. But as athletic as he was, he jumped to the side, and I completely missed him.

It took me a couple of hours to cool off, but later that evening I returned home. Everyone had calmed down by then, and Frankie and I had a long chat. He apologized for slapping me and grabbing the baby. He gave me all the same bullshit that was to become all too familiar during our marriage—flowers and promising he would never do it again. I made it clear to him that night that if it ever happened again, I'm out. I meant it at that time, but I went back on those words numerous times during the coming years.

Nick and Frankie had been friends for a long time. They were both on the surfing team in their separate high schools. We lived near the beach which was the place to be if you're a surfer. All of Frankie's friends were into surfing. It's impossible to calculate how many hours Frankie spent at the beach. It was probably nearly as many as he spent at home, if not more.

I had come from Chicago, and I didn't even know what surfing was, so it was something I learned about by being with Frankie and his friends. Even after he graduated from high school, surfing was still a big part of his life, and things were no different after we married. I loved to watch, film or take photos. In fact, he only quit a couple of years before we were divorced. His whole life, he took every available opportunity to go surfing.

One year while we were married, he came home with his back out on Thanksgiving Day. He had been out on one of the more challenging places to surf. His back took a shot from someone's board. Later, he had another accident that completely blew out his knee, and it required two knee surgeries. One of the side-effects of the injury is that it was the beginning of his Vicodin addiction. He began by taking the medicine for pain, but it's foolish for an addict of any kind to take pain medication.

The injury certainly slowed him down, but he continued surfing for years. When we married, Frankie weighed 165 pounds, and when we divorced, he was closer to 300 pounds. I bring up the issue of his weight because Frankie always tried to make me the scapegoat for all our problems. Appearance was important to him, and that's why he wanted both of us to commit to not gaining any weight—remember the 20-pound rule? I certainly had my share of problems but gaining weight and losing my looks was not one of them.

In January of 1991, our son David was born. By that time, we had moved once again. Dad kept saying that we didn't have enough room for all of us, so we located a house with an extra bedroom. I was almost four months pregnant during the move, and

I started bleeding while standing in the driveway in the midst of boxes and furniture. Frankie hurriedly took me to the doctor when we couldn't get the bleeding to stop.

At that time, being only four months along was not enough to have a sonogram, so we didn't really know for sure what was happening. I was at the hospital for several hours before the bleeding finally stopped, and they sent me home. They instructed me to take it easy and get plenty of bed rest, which was quite tricky since we were in the middle of moving. I was also scheduled to return for several appointments in the coming days.

When the pregnancy was far enough along to make a sonogram possible, it was discovered that I had twins, but one of them was dead. Apparently, it happened the day I had all the bleeding problems. There was a great deal of discussion of what to do, and it was finally determined that since the babies were in separate sacks the best course of action would be to do nothing. In every subsequent sonogram, I could see what was happening and to be honest; it was kind of gross. One baby was alive and growing on schedule. The other was dead and slowly disappearing from the sonogram. I was a fascinating study for the medical professionals at every appointment. In the end, I had natural child birth. Rather than a doctor, I had a midwife scheduled, and the plan was to do an underwater birth. It was a popular fad of the day and was supposed to be a less traumatic beginning for the baby. Because of my experience with the birth of my daughter, I refused to go to the hospital too early. We waited and waited, and I paced around the back yard for hours.

Finally, I woke up Frankie and told him it was time to go.

We hopped in the car and Frankie decided he had to have a disposable camera to capture the event on film. We stopped at the *7-11*, and I almost had the baby in the parking lot. We had waited so long that I didn't have time to clean up or get any pain medication. David was born 30 minutes after we arrived at the hospital. Frankie was in the delivery room, and he passed out as soon as the baby's head crowned.

The doctors were still concerned about the other baby, but there was no evidence he had ever been there. They theorized that the fetus must have disintegrated during the prior months of pregnancy and the remains were passed through the fluids. Doctors kept a close eye on me for the next year to make sure everything functioned well. Everything checked out fine, and it has never been an issue for me since.

The doctor indicated that I was an excellent candidate to have twins with my next pregnancy, which was not good news for Frankie. He took it upon himself to get snipped to make sure it didn't happen. He lied and said it was for me since I had issues with the pregnancy, but he had told me while we were dating, he didn't want any kids. I would have liked to have had more kids. I did put in my two cents about the matter, but in reality, it was his decision. I didn't learn of his plans until the appointment had already been made. I had wished he would have considered what I wanted. I even drove him to the appointment.

Several months later, I overheard him chatting about it with his friends, telling them he could screw anyone around and not get them pregnant. He now had the freedom he needed to be with other women. He cheated on me so many times before we were married that I was not the least bit surprised. Not long after my son was born, Frankie wound up in the ICU at the hospital for four days with atrial fibrulation. He had come home from the races that weekend, not feeling well at all. I made him go in the next morning, and they couldn't get a heart rate on him. Once medication got his heart back to normal, he was told he almost had a stroke. He was only 25 years old, and this was when he started saying he would never live to be 50. Just like his father, but with different reasons I believe.

The house that we had purchased just happened to be the same house where Frankie had grown up. His mother had lost it after her third divorce in 1980 and filing for bankruptcy, and I bought in 1992. He insisted on this home and did not want to see others until we received an answer. Being in that house created more issues for us. Being in the house drug up terrible memories for Frankie. He's never been able to handle current problems much less deal with his past in a healthy manner.

Frankie's former boss, Dan, was a prominent drug dealer in the downtown area. Dan's home was a favorite destination for Frankie. In fact, it's probably accurate to say that he was one of the better customers when it came to drug purchases. When Frankie made the trip at a time when he was watching Catherine, he merely strapped her in a car seat and took her along for the ride. If I had known what he was doing, I would have put a stop to it because it was only a matter of time until it became a problem. Sure enough, the cops knew what was happening at the house and started staking it out on a regular basis. They were hoping to catch customers who would then implicate Dan, so they could shut him down. One evening Frankie and Catherine were late coming home, and I was beginning to worry. I had no idea where they went or what was going on. By the time they finally arrived home unharmed I was pissed off. I laid into Frankie demanding an explanation. He told me how the cops had staked out Dan's place and they pulled him over as he was leaving. He was forced to get out of the car, and they stripped searched him and thoroughly rummaged through his vehicle. They even made him undress my daughter and remove her diaper to make sure the drugs were not hidden on her. Fortunately, they found nothing, and Frankie was permitted to leave. If they had searched a little harder, the would have discovered that he always kept his weed stuffed in the padding underneath the driver's seat.

When we moved into that house, I had no idea that I put my family smack in the middle of drug row. Any kind of drug you wanted could be found on our block. My husband as one of the biggest weed dealers in the area, and he fit in well with the other residents in our neighborhood.

After our son David was born, there were numerous signs of Frankie's rage becoming more and more dangerous. One day I walked into the garage and found him beating a lawn chair into the wall, and another time he was pounding on a tree in the backyard with a baseball bat. Or kicking his foot through the wall in the hallway. Sometimes he would bang his own head on the wall or with his own hands to his head! When I asked him what was going on, all he would say was that he was mad at himself. It happened often enough that a common saying around the house with the kids was, "Don't wake up the grumpy bear." At that point, I was concerned that he would someday turn that anger loose toward me.

One of the reasons women refuse to leave an abusive situation is that the early signs are ignored. Looking back now, it should have been obvious when I saw my husband beating the garage wall with a lawn chair or going to town on the oak tree in the backyard that he was a violent man and that someday it wouldn't be the garage or tree. It's usually only a matter of time before the wife is the object of beating, but it only happens when we ignore the early signs. Another exceptional trait that reared its head about this same time was him introducing me to people as the "bitch". Along with his constant bagging on me about my cigarettes, and always wanted me to dress like a whore, I was doing my best to ignore him and "consider the source" like my mom and grandma always told me.

Before David was born and our move, Frankie took a good job with the city working for the trash company. He brought home tons of porn that people had thrown out in their trash. He also brought in a bunch of other stuff, and we made good money with yard sales on the weekends, selling other people's junk. The entire time we were together, Frankie's routine was to get up at four in the morning, smoke pot, jerkoff in the bathroom, and then out for the day, either working or surfing at the beach. My sister and I call him "wake and bake."

If he wasn't out with other women, he was servicing himself with the aid of his porn. We stopped having sex, not because I wasn't interested but because he didn't need it from me. He used it as a weapon against me. He withheld it except to get what he wanted. We both needed sex, but the difference was that I needed it with him and he found satisfaction in many places. He had his need met with his porn or other women, whichever was convenient at the time. This left me frustrated and feeling used.

Frankie would chase after women, and it didn't matter who they were. I had a few very good friends, and I eventually had to cut ties with them, married or not, in general because he wouldn't quit hitting on them. In fact, I had to stop having any women around period because he couldn't leave them alone. He would sleep with anyone who said yes.

At one point I had a job working for a check cashing company's corporate office. One day I received a call at the office from Frankie. He informed me that he was bringing his boss and bosses girlfriend over to the house. I had met them before, and Frankie talked about them a lot, so I knew they were swingers. Whenever we were around, Frankie's boss would hit on me, and I didn't want that at my own house. I told Frankie I didn't want them around.

He said, "Too late; it's already done."

On the way home, I stopped and bought a large amount of hard liquor. I knew what Frankie was planning and hoping for—he wanted to trade me to his boss for the girlfriend, but said it was for a job promotion. I thought, "That's not happening. My father lives here, and our two young children and this crazy mother-fucker wants to swap his wife in order to sleep with the boss' girlfriend."

The evening began with all of us playing pool in the garage. The reason I bought the liquor was that I made a conscious decision to get as drunk as I could in order to pass out. As the pool game progressed and I drank like a person who had been lost in the desert. I knew the only way to avoid the expectation of having sex with Frankie's boss was to be drunk and lifeless. The next morning, I woke up in my own bed with Frankie next to me. A few minutes later his boss crawled into bed, but nothing happened. Once we got up, we all went to breakfast together. It was evident from the way everyone acted that they had a threesome the night before. I felt nauseous with my kids sitting there next to them! I'm sure the plan was for me to be involved, but I was too drunk, and it didn't happen.

After breakfast, I went on to the office for work. About midway through the morning, I called Frankie and told him to get his shit out of the house. I was finished. He came to the office a short time later, and we had a long talk and then talked, even more, that evening at home. He repeatedly denied everything. It's just impossible for the man ever to admit what sick things he is doing! More lies. Once again, I went back on my word and allowed him to stay. To this day, he will not admit that he slept with all those other women.

My motivation for living was my two kids. I always had to decide what was best for them and that's why I continually let Frankie stay. He would do terrible things, but then he would calm down and be back to his winsome, charming self. I knew that sometimes the harder choice is the best choice. I stayed because I didn't want to get a divorce and force Catherine and David to deal with their father without me being around.

# CHAPTER 5

# Settling in as Married

Things quieted down until 1999, at least as quiet as things can be when you're married to a sociopath and have two young kids. I had the best job of my life working for a school district, making far more money than Frankie. Financially we were doing well—not getting rich but plenty of money to pay the bills and meet the needs of our family. He had been working for the city for 10 years, which is the longest he ever been at a job. However, he was getting more and more pissed off every time he was passed over for a promotion. He had been promoted twice already. Once into the water department, and then again after the incident when the boss had come over that night. One day he snapped and reamed out the City Manager for purposefully promoting only Mormons. That didn't sit well, naturally, which caused him to be looked at more closely by management.

It was during this time that Frankie severely injured his knee while surfing. Between the injury and the surgery, he began using Vicodin. It was foolish for a doctor to prescribe it for a man with a propensity for addiction. Sure enough, it didn't take long before he was hooked on it along with the booze and the weed. I called it his "cocktail". After the outburst with his boss, he was sent for a drug test, and he failed. The city specified that he couldn't come back until he could pass a clean test and needed him to go into the program.

I thought at the time it was lenient of them not to outright fire him, but they gave him a chance to get things right. Would Frankie take advantage of the opportunity? No way! He always lived for the moment and insisted that he couldn't be off the drugs because he didn't know how to do life without drugs.

Also, he was deathly afraid being off drugs and of having dreams, he had said. His boss told him to go home and think about. He came to me for advice. I've always felt like adults need to make their own decisions and should have the sense to take family and other factors into consideration. In my mind, the right thing to do, of course, was to take the time and get clean from the drugs and get back to work. However, I thought it was essential that Frankie make that choice for himself—that's the only way he would be successful. Since I already had two other kids in the house, I refused to tell him what to do. I failed to consider the reality that Frankie doesn't think like most people. He wasn't the least bit concerned about providing for his family or taking responsibility for anyone else. He was only worried about himself.

The next morning, he got up early for his usual bathroom routine with the porn. When it was time for work, he bagged up all of his uniforms and took them with him. He tossed them on the boss' desk and quit. Just like that. The best job he ever had. Apparently, his plan at that point was to go home and start smoking more dope because that's precisely what he did. He cashed in his retirement money which he had accumulated over the past ten years and assumed we would live off that. Idiot!

The money lasted six months, and I was pissed.

"I don't know what you need to do, but get a job," I insisted.

I took some vacation time from work because I felt we needed to get away. I purchased a new car and planned out the trip. I wanted the kids to spend some time with their grandparents before it was too late. Also, I thought it would give us some time to think about what to do next without the usual interruptions. Dad wanted to come so we all piled into the car for a road trip. We made it back to Illinois, but the money ran out after two weeks, so we had to cut the final week from our planned vacation.

While on the trip, I continually encouraged Frankie to think about finding a job. He was probably hesitant because he didn't really want to work, but I blamed it on his drug problem. He kept saying any potential employer would check his background and discover his history with drugs. I suggested that if he was afraid to look for a job because of his drug history then perhaps it was time to move on to someplace else.

Apparently, it was one of the few times when my suggestion got through to Frankie. Once we returned from our two-week vacation, he began seriously looking for a job. He was always afraid of job hunting because potential employers would call his past employers and get a terrible recommendation (at the time this was possible because it was before the law was changed). He broadened his search and even sought out places in other states. Somehow, he found a job in Colorado. It was one of those "Perfect Storm" situations because the company was under some legal pressure to hire non-family members, so they weren't especially careful to check his background. Their most important criterion was a non-family member. Frankie took the job, and we were off to Colorado. This was in the year 2000.

Frankie went ahead of the rest of us to look for a place to live and begin working. I stayed behind to sell the house and tie up other loose ends. I had been around Frankie long enough that I knew he wouldn't stay in Colorado for long. Rather than putting the house up for sale, I rented it, knowing we would be coming back. I was correct—we came back in a year and a half.

Although our stay in Colorado was short, there were some good things about the experience. Having Frankie far away from his friends was good for all of us. However, it didn't take long for Frankie to get anxious about being so far away from Florida. He missed the surfing and the drugs. They did a lot of snowboarding in Colorado which is similar to surfing, but Frankie didn't enjoy it as much. He wanted the warm sand and the ocean waves.

He solved his need for drugs by having one of his Florida friends ship weed to him. He just stuffed it in a coffee can and mailed it to Frankie. With the availability of drugs, things went back to being much like they had been. In fact, once we became more established and met people, he started dealing once again. It will always be true about Frankie that as long as he knows two people, he's going to sell drugs to at least one of them. He never changed. My Dad always warned me he wouldn't change, but it took me awhile before I realized it was true.

In some respects, our marriage was better while in Colorado. I think it was because of his friends not being around and fewer drugs available. Frankie and I didn't have the vicious knock-down-drag-out fights we often had. Both of us were working multiple jobs because the cost of living in Colorado was so high. In fact, that's why we eventually had to leave—it just became too expensive. Frankie was also missing the ocean, so the decision to return to Florida was not that difficult. We lived in a small town situated deep in the Rockies. The town was controlled by crazy people, and we never fit in like we belonged. Neither Frankie nor I were happy with the situation, but had made the best of it.

Moving back to Florida, I went in advance in order to get settled. The priorities were to find work and to get our house back that we had rented out. I stayed in a hotel and fortunately, I got my old job back which was a huge help. Getting the house back was a different story.

The renters were using the house as an odd combination of a meth house and state certified day care. After returning to Colorado to help load up our stuff, we drove back to the Florida with the intention of arriving prior to the moving van. We arrived two days before we were able to get into the house, so we stopped at a motel.

When we pulled into the parking lot, Frankie got out of the truck and walked over to my side just as I was getting out. As soon as I stood up and began to stretch my legs, Frankie's hand came flying directly toward my face. He slapped me so hard that I fell up against the truck. As I worked to regain my bearings, I realized that Dad and our kids were watching. They were all in shock and just stood there, not knowing what to do. I just about lost my mind. It was crazy. I'm sure everyone in the motel heard the commotion, and many of them stood around watching what must have looked like a huge street fight. It was the culmination of a 12-hour ride filled with noise and arguing. Everyone was tired from the trip, and had a long ride with yelling and cussing.

Things finally settled down enough that we were able to get checked into our rooms. Frankie and I had a room to ourselves. I really got into it with him. I didn't want to do it outside in front of Dad and the kids. I went at him verbally for the next two days. As usual, Frankie finally promised he would never lay a hand on me again. Another lie. Once again, I caved and stayed with him.

After a couple of days, it was time to go back to our old house. The renters had trashed everything so horribly that we had to sleep in the driveway for a week. There was a hole in the bedroom the size of a human head, so you can only imagine how that must have occurred. The marble sinks in the bathrooms were busted, and there was damage in every room. We had to do a great deal of work before we could even move into the house.

Now that we were back in Florida, Frankie was back to his old habits. He was still afraid to apply for a job, so I was carrying the finances on two mortgages—where we were living and the one we still hadn't sold in Colorado. Catherine was struggling with anxiety and David, my son, was in bad shape and throwing ridiculous fits that would go on for days. David would throw knives at the door if I looked in just like his Dad did with his brother. He might be in his room a few hours, while hitting his head with his hands, or into the wall before going to sleep. At times he would act out violently just like his father. As I think about it now, David not only learned how to act by watching his father, but it was also a part of his DNA. Remember, Frankie's family has a long rooted history of destructive behavior passed from one generation to the next.

Although I was able to get my old job back, it was classified as a temporary position for the time being. That meant there were no benefits. One day, Frankie showed up with David and banged on the window to my office. When I went outside to see what he wanted, he threw David at me and said, "I can't handle this kid. You need to do something!"

That was quite ironical in my thinking. He couldn't handle his son who was acting just like his father. I'm not sure what he wanted me to do; it was obvious I had no idea how to deal with Frankie.

We faced additional stress trying to get the renters to pay for their damage to our house. They sent several death threats and made frequent drive-byes in front of our house. We were not getting consistent rent from our house in Colorado, so the money was tight. After six or eight months, I put my foot down and insisted Frankie get a job. I didn't care at that point what he did; we needed more income. I told him to clean up his ass, so he could pass a drug test. He did finally get a job before the year was out, but most of his time around the house was spent on porn and drugs. His lack of interest in sex with me continued as well.

Frankie's aunt who lived with his grandmother in Missouri was a highly unusual woman. I liked her. In fact, she was one of the nicest people I've ever known. However, she did some pretty strange things. She was totally into astrology and Mediums. After Frankie's grandmother died, she hooked up with a Medium and made contact with Frankie's father. There's no doubt she truly believed it was him that she spoke with because she said he instructed her to make things right with Frankie concerning the will, and was told this in Danish which the medium did not know. In fact, she took it so seriously that she ended up redoing the will and included Frankie for a sizable sum.

At first, that sounded like great news. We had always lived paycheck-to-paycheck, and now it appeared like we might be able to get ahead financially and remove a great deal of pressure that caused many of our struggles. We had never had extra money, and I had no idea how Frankie would handle things.

From our prior visits with his Aunt, Frankie had learned there was a giant safe under the house. We also knew there was a bunch of gold and silver coins purchased from the money his father had accumulated from selling the company stock. Frankie was convinced the coins that were in that safe was all he wanted in the will. His aunt asked me what I wanted, and I said I would take the house. She replied, "Done!"

A few months after the 9-11 terrorist tragedy, Frankie's aunt called and was frantic. "You have to come," she insisted.

We drove to Missouri as quickly as we could get away and arrived to quite a sight. There was a huge fucking hole in the back yard of the house, and a big crane was dropping a metal cylinder in the hole. It was such a spectacle that a camera crew was filming the entire process. She was installing a bomb shelter. She was so frightened by the terrorist attacks that she decided to make plans to protect us. In addition, she was heavily into prophesy. She told us stories about the Germans who occupied their home during the war and made them slaves. She had seen shelters in Sweden and decided to create a place where we could all be safe when the world comes to an end. It was a bizarre trip, to say the least.

A short time later, Frankie's aunt passed away. Sure enough, we got the house and all the coins, but only what was left. She had spent the money on the shelter and a massive amount of supplies. There was enough inside that hole in the ground to keep eight people alive for a decade, complete with gas masks, body bags, and a state-of-the-art air filtration system.

Frankie was pissed about so much money being spent for all that useless shit. When we returned to Missouri to wrap up the legal stuff surrounding the will, Frankie calculated the money it would take to pay off the debts, repairs on the house, and attorney fees. He estimated it all in his mind and realized he would be forced to dip into the coins she had left him. The house was a dump, and we had to spend a lot of money on probate court. Not only was his aunt living there, but she had also leased out the basement to some students. We had a meeting with them and told them we had to raise the rent. They chose to leave rather than pay extra. Although the house was debt free, he had me take out a $250,000 loan to cover our expenses. Once we secured the loan, he wanted to put the house on the market. He used to yell at me because he never wanted to buy a house in Missouri, and it was my idea to have her give it to me in the will. He wanted the money.

When we returned to Florida, we had a big U-Haul full of shit from Missouri. As we walked in the front door of our house, the first thing we noticed was Catherine and a guy sitting on the couch drinking beer and watching TV. She introduced him as her boyfriend, Jeremy. Frankie lost his mind and started yelling.

While I tried to talk to Catherine, Frankie grabbed Jeremy and dragged him into the backyard. He pinned him up against the wall and threatened him. He told him he didn't like him sitting on his couch, drinking his beer, and watching his TV. Imagine what it was like for this young man. The first time meeting his girlfriend's father and suddenly face to face with a crazy man. It was an ugly scene for all of us. Catherine decided to move to San Francisco with her boyfriend, and I didn't blame her in the least. She wasn't comfortable staying at our house.

After she had been in San Francisco for a short time, I think she felt trapped away from home and began to have panic attacks. When she called and said she wanted to come home, I told her I would fly up and help her drive back. I got up early in the morning to go to the airport and noticed that Frankie had already left the house for the day. When I got to the airport, I called Frankie to tell him what I was doing and what was going on. He lost his mind on the phone.

He said, "We're not doing this again!"

He was referring to a few years earlier and a similar experience with Catherine when she was in Germany. She had panic attacks, and we had to bring her back home. I understood Frankie's anger over the situation. I said, "Ok," hung up the phone and boarded the plane. My seat was in the back of the aircraft near the toilet. As I sat and thought about everything, I decided I wasn't doing this again. I got off the plane before it took off and called Catherine. I told her that her dad was having a fit and I wouldn't be flying out. My best advice was for her to get back together with Jeremy and make it work. Surprise! She didn't listen to my advice. She showed up at my house. Catherine and I had several long talks over the next five days. I did my best to help her feel good about her choices and was eventually able to talk her into returning to San Francisco and her boyfriend. It wasn't that I wanted to get rid of her, but I wanted her to get out of the house and away from her father. A few months later I was able to spend some time with Catherine and Jeremy, and it really was a great trip I did alone without Frankie. They were doing very well.

As I mentioned earlier, I've always had a love affair with cars. Something about them has attracted and kept my attention my entire life. It wouldn't be surprising for me to marry someone with a similar interest—but I didn't. I married a guy who owned a Datsun truck solely for the purpose of hauling his surfboards. With a dream to one day mow two lawns a day, get high and surf. I loved cars, and Frankie loved surfing.

When we were first married, I had a job at a Hyundai car dealership. One of the things I learned in that position was the way dealers handle trade-ins. If a car is over four years old, they will take it as a trade-in, but they won't keep it on the lot. They send it off to auction, often to Las Vegas where there is a huge car auction selling thousands of cars. Prior to shipping the car off, they will usually offer it to any employee willing to pay the amount they spent at trade-in.

One day a man came into the dealership with his granddaughter. He had a restored a '67 Mustang that he had given her, but she didn't want it—she wanted something new. The deal was made, and the man was given $1,950 for the mustang. I jumped at the chance when they offered it to the employees because I knew it had significant value.

At that time, we already owned a couple of cars, and neither Frankie nor I really wanted to keep the Mustang. We replaced a bad tire, stuck a for sale sign in the car window, and parked it in front of our house. A month later sold the car to a kid down the street for $5,000, and Frankie got the bug. Not for cars but for making money by selling cars.

I had a friend at the time who was restoring classic cars and making a great living. Frankie was working for a race team and decided he wanted to begin to flip cars. The money sounded too good for him to pass up. I've always been a car freak, and he's the money freak.

There was no way Frankie and I could make a successful business together with the cars. We had different objectives. I enjoyed having cars and treating them special and enjoying them. All Frankie saw was potential dollar signs. I shouldn't have been surprised, but once Frankie got his hands on all that money from his family's will, money was all he cared about. It was like money had become another addiction for him, and it went well with his booze, drugs, and porn.

# CHAPTER 6

# The Worst Years

Frankie and I were married in 1988. I had no illusions that we would live happily ever after, but I did have hopes we could work through our difficulties, raise our children, and enjoy life together. As I've already documented, we had problems from the beginning, but I always held on to hope that we could make it work. Even if I had to stick around for the kid's sake, I was willing to do that if necessary.

However, after almost 20 years of struggles things really started to spiral downward. Even though I was committed to staying with the family and making things work for the kids, it took a toll on me. I fell into a serious depression.

Each day was a struggle just to get up and do the things required. I hated the marriage. I hated my life. There was nothing in this for me. I had no one looking after me and my needs.

In 2006 I told Frankie that I was finished, and I was getting a divorce. He did his usual act of turning on the charm, begging me to explain why, as if he didn't see any problem. Every time he abused or harmed me, the apologies and promises never to do it again followed immediately. The years of lies, cheating, porn, drugs, neglect, sexual needs not being met, and all the kinds of abuse there is. It took me a long time to accept the fact that he was never going to change. For 20 years we had been fighting about our lack of sex and porn, and he still couldn't see a problem.

Yet, I'll admit it was my fault because I stayed, and I let him stay. I didn't get the divorce and always allowed the family to talk me into trying to help him out. Everyone knew he was the problem and everyone wanted to help him. I had one child off in college and the other one in high school by then. I finally told him that I was going to make his life a living hell, start treating him as he had me, and become the bitch he always introduced me to people as. At that point, he began to compromise, and it seemed as if he wanted to try at least to make things better. That's when he agreed to work on things with a counselor. However, it didn't take long to discover that he would not be able to follow through on these promises. At least not in the way I had hoped it would be.

Before we began therapy, I moved into Catherine's bedroom. Frankie and I hadn't slept together for years. I slept in the car, the garage, the floor, back porch, just wherever I could find a spot. When he slept, I was afraid to wake him. I crawled into bed with him one night and got a fist in my face. Like my Mom, one of the worst things you could do was wake him up. I spent 20 years trying to get him to notice that I was his wife.

Six months would go by without any sex between us. He withheld it because he knew it was one of the things I wanted. At one point, early in our marriage, he gave me a dildo and asked me to use it rather than bother him. Even when we did have sex, he would simply satisfy himself and then roll over and go to sleep. I never understood because while dating, and before my son was born, our sex life was really good! I spent many nights in the bed next to him crying about living with someone who doesn't fucking care.

Our first counselor told me that I was living in a love-less marriage. I guess I knew it already, but it was tough to hear the words. I was carrying the load for two and I was tired of being sad and lonely.

In addition to dealing with Frankie's shit, I still had kids and my Dad. David was having problems in school at the same time. He inherited his father's rage which caused severe problems for him. He had been in a fight in grade school when I got a call to come to the principal's office. She had told me David wouldn't stop beating this boy until four grown men finally pulled him off. She recommended I get him help for his rage and get some medication. He had drove himself to high school in a jeep that we purchased for him. The school parking lot was always full, so he parked across the street at a nearby business. I never learned all the details, but there was a guy, an adult at least 21-years-old, on the school grounds harassing my son. I don't know if they did drugs together or anything about their relationship.

This man had been harassing my son for a couple of weeks. David was at that age where he didn't share everything with his Mom as he did when he was younger, so I was not aware of the problem. The man followed David to his jeep. He didn't have a car but was riding a skate-board. David ran into him and knocked him down. When David had to stop at the light at the intersection, the man caught up with him and began pounding on the jeep. At that point, David ran into him again.

I was called to the school, and the police were involved as well. David was going to be expelled. I couldn't protect him anymore like I did in the past when I worked for the school district he was in. He was signed up for alternative education. However, that was delayed because of a motorcycle incident. Let me explain. One of the ridiculous things Frankie did after getting the money was purchase a motorcycle—a Harley, to be exact.

Not only did he get one for himself, but bought a motorcycle for our son. Frankie and I had been in a motorcycle accident back in high school, and I wasn't fond of the idea of David riding one. I wasn't able to stop Frankie from giving it to him, but I did insist on safety equipment, and I signed David up for a safety class. I actually attended the course with him and really enjoyed it. I don't plan to ride one on a daily basis anytime soon though.

On one of his first trips without supervision, David headed off in front of his friend on his motorcycle. He had only been gone a short time when his friend Bill came to our house and shouted that David had been in an accident and was hurt. When I got there, it was apparent he had run straight into a block wall. He was still lying on the ground when I arrived. I was so thankful he was wearing a helmet or else his skull would have been split wide open. Although he avoided a serious head injury, other parts of his body were in bad shape. His right hand was mangled, and the motorcycle peg went through his foot like a sword, and it was a mess. David was loaded into an ambulance and taken to the hospital where he had surgery at 1:00 in the morning.

Another time that David's rage came out was when Frankie and I were having a heated argument in the kitchen one evening. David decided that he was now man enough to take on his Dad and that it was up to him to save Mom. This being not long after my son and dad had come in one night to get Frankie off me while I was being strangled. There comes the point when every young man needs to prove that he's stronger and tougher than his father, but this was not David's time. It didn't turn out well for him because Frankie had him pinned on the floor in a second and a half. Once again, I had to rescue my son. That was the first time he ever stood up to Frankie, and I'm sure it was also the last time.

We managed to get David through school, but it was evidence of something I had always feared—he was going to be like his father. The craziness that was in Frankie's family history was being passed on to another generation, and it broke my heart to see my son plagued with the same issues.

Another year rolled around, Frankie's "cocktail" was in high gear. Between the booze and the drugs, there was no way we could have any kind of decent marital relationship. If I had to list Frankie's priorities, it would probably be in this order: himself, drugs, porn, surfing, and if you go far enough down the list you get to the family and me. We were not having much success getting him off street drugs and having the bipolar meds work well, which made it impossible for us to improve our relationship. I had always thought drugs were the problem, but I was wrong!

It was also the year that I discovered Frankie's girlfriend. I had actually met her earlier when we were doing an engine swap in our driveway one day. He introduced her as a friend from the beach, and he told her to come by the house, and we would show her how to change the oil in her car. She was only twenty-one or twenty-two, and it was somewhat suspicious when she showed up wearing a mini-skirt. That's not an outfit one would wear to learn how to change the oil in your car.

I knew at that moment what was going on, but I didn't address it at the time. We were busy doing the engine swap, so I didn't want to get into it. Also, I knew that no matter what I said, he would lie. Even though everyone knew something was true, Frankie had this amazing ability to lie and act as if everyone else was wrong. It's like he actually believed his side of the story and everyone else was wrong. I suspect that's part of his sociopathology. When he wants something to be true and gets it in his mind that it is true, it's impossible to convince him otherwise, even when you show him obvious facts.

A month or so later, the mailman delivered a letter addressed to him from the girl in the driveway. It was a five-page love letter. When I approached Frankie with the letter to ask what was up with his girlfriend, of course, he denied their relationship. He was never going to admit any shit—ever.

In one of the huge fights that always broke out between us, he ended up storming out of the house and took all the gold coins with him to work. I knew he took them in order to make sure I didn't do anything with them. Who does that—carry a heavy load of gold coins around on a motorcycle? When I realized he had taken the coins, I called him at work and accused him of being insane. He was carrying a shit load of gold coins on his Harley. I threatened that if he didn't want to straighten out our disagreement on the phone I would come to his work and it wouldn't be pretty.

At the time, he worked at a water treatment plant that employed thousands of people, and he didn't want me throwing a fit in front of them. To put a stop to it, Frankie went to his boss and told him that I was coming to the office with a gun. He accused me of making serious threats. Although I didn't know it at the time, Frankie's employer turned me in to Homeland Security because I was threatening the workplace with a gun. It's ironic because, at the time, we didn't even have any guns at our house. It was a long time before I learned of this lie.

In the spring of that year, Frankie was sent to Tampa for testing for a Grade 5 Water Treatment certification. His employer paid for everything, and Frankie knew how to take advantage of that perk. He was supposed to be gone for three days. The first night he called, and it was apparent he was drunk. He was especially excited because his boss, who was married, by the way, had a hooker coming to the hotel room. I had met his boss' wife before, and Frankie told me that every time he leaves town he gets a hooker.

From that call, I could read the handwriting on the wall. The next day I tried to call and got no response. By the third day with no contact, I was really getting pissed. When he finally called, he became enraged and hung up on our conversation. A short time later he showed up at home. I found him in the garage, and when he saw me, he started laughing at me.

He said, "You suck in bed."

I didn't bother even to ask if he had paid for a hooker. I know he did! It didn't matter if I asked or not since he would lie either way. He would just spin my words, and it would turn into more horrendous fights.

Later on though, there was an especially vicious argument in the kitchen. It started like all of our arguments. I was furious with his disrespect for our marriage, and wondering if I might get some disease from his cheating! He was on his bipolar medication and still self-medicating with other drugs and booze. During this particular skirmish, he pushed me down on the kitchen floor tile and busted my tailbone. Frankie stormed out of the house like always. In fact, he kept an air mattress and other necessary articles in his car just in case he needed to get away for a few days. Or maybe he did this to hide from the cops in case I finally called them.

My daughter had to take me to the ER. After the initial exam, the doctor came back into the room with forms and said they had noticed the giant handprints on my arms and that I needed to inform the police. They also advised me that if I was not willing to report the incident, and have him arrested, then they would refuse to treat me. Catherine was in the lobby, and I wasn't sure what to do. She was only 18, and I didn't want to involve her, so I walked away without treatment.

Frankie had been seeing psychiatrists and counselors for years when he was young, but I wanted to go to a marriage counselor for the first time. He continued to go to his shrinks, but I wanted to go to someone who would help both of us. Hopefully with the sex issue or porn. The first counselor we chose had a fabulous reputation. She possessed several advanced degrees and was well respected among her peers. Her first position was at UCLA as a research scientist where she studied marijuana. This was back in the 1960's when it first became popular. Her research involved chimpanzees and she observed how using too much weed turned their frontal lobe to black mush. She talked about how perplexed she was that it was ever legalized. Her familiarity with weed meant that she immediately knew Frankie was stoned when he walked in the door. Right up front, she told Frankie to stop smoking dope or get out of her office. We left. Needless to say, Frankie was not interested in using her for counseling.

Hoping to have some time together doing something we both loved, we booked a trip to Las Vegas to a drag race and car show. I decided to bring my car for the race and let Frankie drive it.

To everyone's surprise, he won the event. It was the first time he had ever driven.

At those shows, the racers who have been eliminated and no longer driving, usually pack up their stuff and go home. By the evening of the final day, the only thing left to do is the championship race, presentation ceremony, and photo shoot. Since Frankie won the whole damn thing, we were there until late in the evening. Frankie was at the pinnacle of the most wonderful thing that had ever happened to him. He was on top of the world, filled with excitement and adrenaline.

We returned to the hotel where we were staying. My car was being towed with a wagon we had specially built for that purpose. It was a special car. In fact, it won 3rd prize at the Vegas car show the previous year. We parked the trailer and wagon in the gravel lot behind the hotel.

Later in the evening while returning from the racetrack, Frankie noticed that someone, probably a truck driver, had chipped the paint on the car with the loose gravel. He went ballistic. He stormed through the casino cussing toward everyone. At the front desk, he made an idiot of himself. The best way to describe it is to say he was insane. It's surprising that the police never showed up to take him away—he was out of control. Our friend who was with us, just left, which was typical behavior when Frankie was on the loose.

I returned to the hotel room to wait it out. I didn't want to deal with him, and I knew he would eventually calm down and come back. Sure enough, when he was finally done, he came up to the room. He was still angry and ranting.

I started laughing and said, "You just went from the high point of your life, and ten minutes later you go into an idiotic rage. There's more fucking going on here than simply being bipolar. Your pills aren't working."

I had witnessed a lot of shit with Frankie over the years, but I had never seen a change happen so quickly. Somehow, he seemed to be getting worse all the time. I learned over the years that Frankie could change like that in an instant. He could go from the nicest person in the world to the angriest, nastiest man you have ever seen in the blink of an eye. Once you get to know him, you can see it on his face. More precisely, you can tell from the way his eyes change colors. When they turn pitch black, it's time to get out of the way or hang on for a wild ride.

During one of the times he attempted to stop smoking weed, after our divorce discussion, he called me in to the bedroom for a talk. When I came in the room he was crying. This didn't happen often, so I asked what was going on. He said, "God had showed him how awful he had been to me in a visualization". He said how sorry he was, and asked me for a hug, and I hugged him as he was still crying. Before the hug was over, he started to say, "And I really hate the way you dress, the way you talk, and that you like guy stuff". That was such a quick switch, I looked at him and the tears had stopped, and he looked intent on harm again. I just never knew when the change would occur, but they were getting faster and more intense for me. Even with the new medications, Frankie was a whack job. His mother told me once that the money is what really changed him. It took what was already an evil in his life—his mental instability and blew it out of proportion. We had always been a family that lived from paycheck to paycheck. We had the expense of kids, we haphazardly landed union jobs, but we never had a great deal of money.

In fact, several years earlier in 2004 before my daughter was graduating from high school, we were filling out college applications, and I remember that we were making a lot of money together. I was actually making more than Frankie in addition to having excellent benefits. However, when I did quit my union job, it changed our financial situation and allowed her to get scholarship money for college. She chose a private school which cost $30,000 per year. Even with that much money, we weren't doing great. Frankie loved to spend. He always spent the money as soon as it came in. When the kids were little, I would hide money from him to pay bills before he spent it, and bought gifts year round and hid them before he saw I had spent money. He bought cars like they were going out of style. After a short time, he would get bored and buy something else. He had new surfboards and everything else that caught his attention. One of our biggest expenses was his drug usage. That expense was huge. Although he continued dealing, he didn't bring in enough to cover his own drug expenses.

Often it was crazy, unexpected things. One day I received a call that he was in Tampa getting his eyes fixed. I had no idea he was planning that, but he spent $5,000 just like it was trip to a convenience store. However, I don't think the money changed him. Instead, it just gave him bigger opportunities to be the fuck up he had always been. What it did do was encourage people to stick with him, even after he treated them like shit. People saw him as a source of money, and we all know that many people will do anything for money.

Once again, we returned to Missouri to tend to the house. On a trip alone, he wanted to get cable for the tv, or to have something else to do besides spend time with me. I had asked about sex in the evening and was turned down immediately by a sudden rash he had. Later in the night, I saw him through his blinds, we slept apart as each room only had a twin bed, jacking off to porn on the tv! I got up there and started a huge fight. Of course, it went nowhere, as they all seemed to, and Frankie always got his way. It seemed we were there almost every other month for quite some time. As I noted earlier, on our trips he liked to have a drug buddy come along, someone to party with. On several of the trips he brought his friend Dan, and occasionally I would fly in my sister, so I wouldn't be alone.

We had huge raging fights at least once a week, sometimes more often. I remember one in particular. The shrinks and I were trying to wean him from his drug cocktail, starting with the Vicodin. Also, we wanted to get him off the porn. The shrinks were working to help us get back together sexually. In hindsight, it might be that we were trying to solve too many things at once, but it wasn't like we hadn't tried them all before.

He ended up leaving the house and just took off. In a sense, having Frankie walk away from a fight is better than experiencing the violence if he stays. About a half an hour later, we noticed that he had not returned yet. He had walked off without his wallet or anything, maybe just to cool off. By this time it was 1:00 in the morning.

I finally decided to try and find him, and after a short search, I located him downtown. I was able to talk him into the car after about 15 minutes and brought him back home. The next day,

he and I started up the argument again. Once again, he went into a full rage, and I wasn't sure what to do. He started to attack me like he was going to rape me, screaming, "Is this what you want?" He was overreacting to our talk about my wanting to have sex. I really wasn't expecting him to jump into that mode. He knew I had been raped as a young teenager and it still bothered me. He did stop before it escalated, but it threw me off for the weekend. I have no idea where it came from; perhaps it was a game he played with hookers. Fortunately, I never saw it again.

I wasn't sure what to do with him. Finally, he left. In fact, he left the state and returned home. It wasn't unusual, most of the time because out of my frustration I would ask him to leave. After most of our huge fights he would go, it had happened several times before. I called and asked if he was going to return and pick me up, but he wasn't interested. I phoned my daughter and asked her if she would like to come to Missouri and get me before I booked a flight. She had not been to Missouri to see the house yet, so it was an opportunity for her. She came, and we had a fantastic weekend then drove back home together.

Once back at home, nothing had changed. In the fall we quit going to marriage counseling because he wouldn't do any of the work suggested by the counselor, no matter what she asked us to do.

We had a couple of discussions during the year about starting a business of some kind. I owned a couple of classic cars, one of them had been in a movie. I noticed an ad for Budget Rental Cars and that they offered classic cars to rent in our area. I also met several people who owned classic vehicles and leased them to movie studios and others who needed them short term. After some research on the Internet, I realized it was being done all over the country. It was an idea I had thought about doing some day, but when Frankie got his inheritance, he decided to give it a try.

He called one day from a muffler shop near our house. He made a deal with the owner to get the vacant shop in the back and wanted me to help finalize the arrangement. I had no idea we were actually going to do something about using a shop. I had suggested we take the rest of the money to pay off the house we were living in and pay off the loan from Missouri, which would make us completely debt free, but that was of no interest to Frankie.

He said he wanted to start the business with cash. The economy was not good, and it seemed like a terrible time to go out on a whim and start a new business, even with cash.

He insisted he wanted to do it and was adamant that I go in there and make a cash deal with the old man. I went in a talked to the man and secured a good deal. We signed a year's lease for the shop space. We spoke to my friend who was great with cars, made him an offer to come work with us and he took it. We got the shop set up, and the goal was to rent the cars, but my concerns were correct, it was an awful time to start the business. We were restoring classic cars, and Frankie began buying them faster and faster. We were doing complete restorations, and the cars piled up more quickly than we could restore them. When we finally closed the shop, we had sixteen cars.

As the end of the year approached, our lives were still consumed with constant arguing. It was usually me bagging on him about the lack of sex, porn, or drugs. Over the years he had gone from magazines around the house to constantly watching movies on the computer. Earlier when I wanted to divorce, I had found his pornography files on our laptop, and he went into a rage and busted the computer over a bed post! Our horrible fighting was getting more and more severe with the passing of time. One night we took the argument into the bedroom. He launched up from the bed and began to strangle me. Dad and David both came rushing into the bedroom to peal him off me. Once again, he grabbed a bag and took off in his wagon. I didn't see him for the next five days.

As usual, Frankie came back home, and everything continued unchanged. At the end of the year, we purchased tickets for a Metallica show. It's one of my favorite bands, and I was very excited since I had never seen one of their shows live. We drove downtown for the concert., but the opening band was a no-show. That meant there was a lot of time to kill, two extra hours. Everyone kind of wandered around outside looking for things to do. We chatted with three guys while waiting in the line to get beer.

A short time later, Frankie heard they were shutting down beer sales at 9:00, so he wanted to get back in line and stock up before the show started. After that, I'm not sure what happened. I remember standing outside and continuing to chat with the guys we met in line. By the time Frankie returned, I had finished the beers that were sitting on the shelf, and the three guys took off. I remember hearing the first few songs of the concert, but nothing after that.

Apparently, I was unconscious for 15 hours. Someone hit me with a date rape drug, but I don't know who. I'm surprised I lived through the evening. Frankie told me that I fell into the crowd in front of us and he had to help walk me out from the show to the car. He didn't take me to a hospital because he said that he was drunk. Instead, he took me home and left me sleeping in the driveway with a heater running.

When I woke up, I took a shower, dressed, and went to the shop. When I arrived, Frankie was already there working. He seemed adamant it was the guys outside that had drugged me, and I should thank him for bringing me home. That's when Frankie clued me in on what had happened the night before. He told me a story of me waking a few times for only a brief moment enraged. That I kicked him, the car, then I would pass out again in only minutes. I had been drugged, and Frankie thought he was doing me a favor by letting me sleep it off on the driveway.

The effects of being drugged that evening didn't end after I woke up in the driveway. There was much more to come.

One year later, Metallica brought their show back to town and I wanted to go again since I missed the previous year. I made it through the concert this time, but when we got home, I wasn't feeling well. I was sick enough that I decided to give up alcohol until things got better. However, after a week of no drinking at all, I started vomiting, and I couldn't quit. It finally got so bad that I asked Frankie to call the EMT's. They checked me over and said I needed to go to the emergency room. Rather than the expense of an ambulance, Frankie drove me there himself.

As soon as we arrived, they started the tests. It didn't take long before they reported that my organs were beginning to shut down. When the doctor who came into to see me, bitched at Frankie for waiting so long to bring me to the hospital when I should have been brought in a year ago! The diagnosis was pancreatitis, and I was told that it was a life or death situation. They started treatment immediately, and it was a grueling process. I gradually rallied and was able to get out of the hospital a few days before Christmas. At that point, I needed to stop drinking. I did, and I distinctly remember the doctors gave me five stars when I did it.

The doctor blamed my sickness on the Rohypnol that I had been given the previous year. I had continued drinking for the entire year since the incident not thinking it was a problem. I'm not an alcoholic, but I do enjoy drinking alcohol. If I had known it was going to contribute to such a severe problem I would have stopped.

I have no idea who slipped the drug into my beer. It could have been Frankie; I just don't know. Sometimes I think he might have been trying to kill me, but goddam it, I lived through it. I will admit that it hurts my heart to think that was a possibility.

# CHAPTER 7

# Divorce and Beyond

In 2013, an event occurred between Frankie and I that was one of the most ridiculous, obnoxious experiences of my life. At the time, we thought he had stopped using street drugs, and the doctors had correctly regulated his medication. Apparently, that wasn't true.

We were in Vegas, and he was crazier than bat shit at a car show. I brought in some relatives and friends to help out with the logistics of the show. We were just getting our business up and running, and it was vital that we do things right and make a good impression. During one of his crazy moments, we got into it as usual. He took off in his car, and no one had any idea where he was going.

Usually, during these episodes, he would spend the night sleeping in his car, and that's what I suspected he was doing. Instead, he stayed up all night gambling at the casino, or maybe got a hooker. My cousin saw him driving through the parking lot in the wee hours of the night, and a few hours later he called everyone going to the track for the day, except me, and invited them to breakfast, his treat. Apparently, he had won some more money than I had seen the night before. Even though I wasn't invited, my cousin called again to see what was going on. I had joined to go to work the business and told him we should discuss it later. After things calmed down, I told Frankie that we needed to talk about the events of the previous night.

We had the conversation in the car because I don't like to have private discussions in public places. I told him that when he takes off drunk in a strange city, I worry about him. I was honest and wanted to let him know that I cared about him and what was going on with him, and I didn't sleep a wink worried. I might be hard to believe after

45

reading this much of my story, but I really did love the guy. There were many things he did that I hated, but as paradoxical as it might sound, I loved him and wanted the best for him. That explains why I started crying as I shared my feelings and concern.

Frankie laughed when he saw me crying. Not just a quiet snicker or simple chuckle. He laughed out loud, and I lost it. Throwing open the car door, I jumped out and walked back to the tent where my cousin was selling tickets at the show. Just as I arrived at the tent, Frankie ran up and started kicking the shit out of me with his steel toed boots while I was sitting in a chair. There was nothing I could do to stop him because he's so much bigger than me. About 300 people stood around watching—doing nothing. I didn't even know what I did to set him off.

Later, I discovered that when I slammed the car door, the window that had been open, broke inside the door. When the glass shattered, Frankie went ballistic and attacked me in front of everyone. When he finished, he walked back to the car and drove off. My cousin, who was right there when it happened was freaking out—not so much because I had been beaten but because her purse and tickets for the show were in the car. Frankie was gone for the rest of the day.

I pulled myself together and cleaned up as much as possible and worked the auto show the rest of the day. A short time later I was talking to a friend who told me that Frankie was on the other side of the parking lot sleeping in his car. However, all my friends made it clear that they didn't want to get involved. I walked across the lot to the car. My shin where I had been kicked the hardest was swollen and sore. I acted apologetically toward Frankie so I could get the show tickets and my cousin's purse.

Anyone else would have been scared shitless that he was going to jail for beating up a woman or perhaps someone would come after him. Not Frankie. About 5:00, after the racing was complete, he rolled over in the wagon to the tent where I was working and demanded, "Get in the fucking car!"

He came at me again on the way up to the hotel room where we all had to change and shower. I had gone to find him to use the shower, and he was in the bar gambling again. Out in the hallway I just sat and cried! I had him go with my cousin and her friend to dinner as I just was emotionally drained. My cousin's friend filled me in on my cousin's intentions of getting with Frankie, and she does that with all men including her friends' boyfriend. I tried to stay calm and cool throughout the remainder of the weekend because it was important for my business. I was trying to build relationships and didn't want them to know about our personal problems. It was not easy with Frankie because every night was like a roller coaster ride, up one minute and down the next. He went from half-assed ok to the next minute like stink on shit and threatening me.

When the events of Vegas were finished, Frankie and I rode home together. During the trip, I laid into him for at least an hour or more. Once we arrived, he dropped me off at the house and then went to Home Depot where he purchased a lock and key. When he came back home, he locked himself in our spare room and wouldn't speak to me, look at me, or acknowledge me in any way. This went on for a couple of months.

Prior to this event, we had celebrated our 25th wedding anniversary. He booked a hotel nearby, and we just did a little walking around and dinner. We had a quicky for sex, then he showered and went to sleep saying he didn't feel good. I talked to my daughter a few hours on the phone, then woke him up. I wanted to be pleasured as I didn't earlier before he went to sleep. He got pissed and a huge fight arose. Just because I wanted our anniversary to be good and enjoyable for me too.

It was an awkward situation because my daughter Catherine had recently moved back home. I worked hard in the business, trying to make it work and keep the family together as much as possible. It was a tough time with Frankie locked in a room away from any interaction. It sounds crazy when I think about it now because it was crazy.

One day, a friend who helped out with the business was at the house. I overheard him talking with Frankie in the front yard. I heard Frankie say that he had decided he didn't want to be married any longer. After the call from our friend who is a lawyer, I had gotten one for myself. I was advised by both the shrinks and the attorneys, to get him arrested to go into an institution to be really looked at for diagnoses to further know Frankie. When the police receive four or more calls in a year, they get a four day lock up. In many of our fights, Frankie would break my phone for this reason. He had known of this law as well. About that same time, I discovered that during the Vegas trip, Frankie was hitting on my cousin and she enjoyed it. In many ways, she's just like him.

The night Frankie was out gambling in Las Vegas, he won several thousand dollars. He hadn't said anything about it and kept it all to himself. When I came home one day, Catherine was all excited because he told her he was going to use the money to buy her a new car. I'm sure he did it to make me angry as well as win her approval. Catherine already owed us $5,000, and the last thing and I wanted to do was provide more money. I knew I had no say and couldn't stop it, so I went with her to the dealership to at least help her get a good deal.

Our work restoring classic cars received some great publicity from national magazines. They ran several articles about it throughout the years. They invited us to travel to Carlisle, Pennsylvania for a large show that would be great for our business. Frankie and I loaded up the car and trailer to make the trip. My mother warned me about going as she reminded me that Frankie frequently left me stranded when we were off on trips, and of course about the fights. We slept in different rooms some nights, and had some outrageous fights. One day while traveling, he wanted to stop to eat. I agreed but I wasn't hungry so I said I was going to call and check on my dad. He got out of the truck and started cussing at me because I wasn't going inside with him. Then he yelled, "Get in the fucking truck". I did, and the fight was on. During this one, I was digging about the porn. He answered at one point, "They like me there. They give me something you could never give me."

As I let that sink in to my vision, I said, "You are really a sick bastard. They don't even know that you're alive. It's not real." I will say though, it was enlightening to know his state of mind finally.

We made the trip, and both of us survived the many hours together on the road.

The day after we got back home, we had a major fight. I started this one, as a lot of them, because I was so exhausted by his refusal to do anything to help our marriage. Even after years of counseling and numerous shrinks, all he still cared about was himself. My sister, who had been staying at the house while we were gone to take care of Dad, was still around. She had a friend come with her, and she was staying in the spare bedroom.

The morning after we arrived at home, Frankie got up and walked across the hall to my sister's friend's room. The door didn't have a lock, so he simply pushed it open and went in unannounced. Sitting on the bed, he began to stroke her hair and rub her head, but she pretended to be asleep. She ignored his presence for several minutes and he finally gave up and left the room. As soon as he departed, she got out of bed, packed her bag, and quickly got in the car. Later, when I took my sister to the airport, she told me what had happened.

That afternoon, Frankie came home from a session with one of his shrinks. We were sitting on the front porch playing cards and drinking when he walked through and asked me to do the homework for him that had been assigned by the shrink. I didn't say a word about my sister's friend because I knew he would just lie and I didn't want to hear it. Rather than agreeing to do the work, I told him I was done helping him. The fight was on, and he headed off to his bedroom and I followed.

Once in the bedroom, he stripped down and jumped into bed. He had a breathing machine that he used when sleeping, and he grabbed the mask and put it over his face and laid down on the bed. I was pissed and wanted to finish the conversation, so I snatched up the machine intending to drag it outside. Frankie grabbed it from my hands and pushed me to the floor with a quick shove. Then he latched on to my arm and hair and pulled me out of the room into the hall. He stormed back into the bedroom and slammed the door shut. I heard him cussing and throwing shit around the room.

I wasn't going to let it end with my lying on the floor and him just skipping out again. The space next to his bedroom was where we kept the pool table, so I grabbed a pool cue from the rack to use as protection. Then I peeked in the door. I had a firm grip on the door handle, and suddenly, the door was flung open, and he grabbed the cue. He then got me to the ground again and dragged me away from the door by my hair. As soon as I made it to my feet, I went to get a machete I kept around for safety. Clutching it close to me, I parked myself in a cubby in the dining room waiting to see what he would do next. I feared for my life.

Frankie came out of his bedroom and paced back and forth in front of me like a lion stalking his prey while looking for car keys. After a few minutes, he began to yell and cuss. I just ignored him as much as possible, still clutching to the machete. When he finally left, he grabbed my purse with all my stuff inside and took it with him. The next day I learned that he was at a friend's house. When we did have the chance to talk, he got in my face and insisted that I should have expected this to happen. Once again, it was always my fault.

Before proceeding to the next part of the story, I need to stop and explain something about myself. I'm a very spiritual person. I have been all my life. When I was young, I became a born-again Christian. It was at one of those "end of days" movies where you are asked to choose which line you want to join—heaven or hell. I was freaked out and went home and got saved. However, during my drug years I gave it up, but then later when I was pregnant with Catherine, I did it again. One of the reasons I stayed with Frankie was because of my religious mindset—forgive and move on.

I'm convinced that much of Frankie's problem must be handled through the spiritual realm. We tried the medical approach with almost every type of medication in existence. We also tried psychological, visiting numerous shrinks who never found the answer. Consequently, I had turned to the spiritual and invited a Medium to come to the house and help.

I described the problem to her, and she insisted on coming to the house to evaluate what was occurring. This was during one of the times he had locked himself in a room. She thought it was essential to have access to every room, so I told Frankie that she was coming and that she needed access to the room. He agreed to unlock the room and be there when she arrived.

She was scheduled to arrive at noon, and Frankie left the house about thirty minutes earlier. When I explained to the Medium that he left, she started laughing and said, "Of course he did."

What I didn't know was that she had paid a visit spiritually the night before. She had met Frankie, and she told me that he didn't like her coming. The minute we walked into the house, she pointed at Frankie's room and she blurted out, "There it is right there!"

The room was what had previously been our media room, complete with the TV, computer, and audio equipment. He slept in there, and like he always did, every morning at four, I could hear him jacking off. When the Medium entered the room, she pointed out a spot and told me there was a portal opened for spirits right there. She went on to say that he's opened it up and there are about twenty others in the room.

She went on to explain that there was a particular entity, she actually stated demonic, that has been with him since he was a kid, around 12 years old she said, and there was nothing she could do about it. It wasn't going away. She added that it didn't matter where we went, it would always be with him. That explained the craziness while we were on our trips and traveling. We walked through the house further, and she began cleansing. Just as she was finishing, Frankie walked in, greeted her, and went to the back yard and sat down.

As Frankie walked away, the Medium asked, "Did you see that?"

I told her I saw something, and she identified it as the entity that won't go away.

When Frankie came out of his room, about three hours after the Medium left, he was an entirely different person. It was a trip—so bizarre. He was the nicest guy I've ever seen. He was apologetic and told me he was taking me out to dinner. He instructed me to get dressed up because we were going to have fun. He indicated that he wanted to hear everything the Medium and I talked about because he thought it was fantastic.

As we travelled to the restaurant, I asked if he would move back into the bedroom and take the lock off the door, and he said he would. We went to a restaurant where Catherine, our daughter, worked. It's a beautiful place, and they have blues and jazz in the evenings. Frankie and I had both "lawyered up" prior to this. I had received a call from his lawyer, our friend, and told for me to get one. I informed him of all the things that had been going on. He was totally shocked. I don't know if Frankie was trying to show Catherine he was trying to improve or what, but he acted like a new man. Looking back over the situation, I think his attorney had probably told him it was not in his best interest financially to be divorced. That would explain why he was so nice—always looking out for himself.

It's an extremely rare occasion for Frankie to cry. I've seen it no more than four times during our time together. When he does break down, it always looks authentic, but I'm not sure. While we were in the car that night, I told a story about when we took the kids camping. I looked over at him, and he was bawling like a baby. He said that he couldn't remember the past. He doesn't recall any of the experiences together as a family. In fact, he claimed that he couldn't remember the good or the bad stuff. I thought it was a result of the years of heavy drug use. He called his weed "the forgetter" and reminded customers to watch their keys so not to lose them.

The other fact that Frankie can't remember stuff makes perfect sense to me. He has been diagnosed by psychologists as having multiple personalities or dissociative identity disorder. This isn't something I made up. It comes directly from the shrinks who have spent hours talking to Frankie and trying to understand. It's one of the areas they asked me to help them understand.

When he was a kid at school, probably in grade school or junior high, someone like a bully approached him. Frankie had got in to a fight with this bully at school, and no one else knows anything about it, but Frankie thought he had killed the kid. He told me that he made a deal or a promise that he would never do it again. I'm not sure what it all means, but I've learned in my spiritual quest, that Native Americans have a tradition that suggests at that moment, he lost his soul. It was about that time that he started creating different identities. Also, at about the same time, he sometimes felt suicidal, and began to use street drugs.

There was a second time he locked himself in a room. This time the other spare room about six months after coming out of the other one. We had plans to do the Phoenix show the next week, and I had been working fulltime but given the time off in advance for the show. I managed to get him out of that room the day of his appointment with a friend who was a medium. He had seen one before to ask about his dad. She began by telling him how intuitive I was and he should listen to me, then spend twenty minutes on "taking everything out from under his rug". She stopped by asking to hold his hands.

Her eyes got real big as she looked over at me. She said, "You have a lot of energy but none of it is good." I'm not sure what it all means, but I do know that personally, I've seen and experienced at least four different personalities. I had not heard the term dissociative identity disorder before, but I did know of his multiple personalities. The shrinks mentioned this is one of reasons for memory lapses as one personality may not recall what another personality has done! The first is the original guy that I met and knew back in the day. He was the "surfer dude" who was merely going through life waiting to catch the next wave. I haven't seen that guy in many years.

The second personality I've seen, far too often, is the psycho evil guy. This is the Frankie that just cannot tell the truth. He lies about everything, even when caught red-handed in a lie. In fact, if he's caught, the lie merely gets bigger, and he gets more determined to maintain his veracity.

The third person is the fake person; the one who says, "Hey, how's it going," whenever he greets you. He the bullshit guy, the front man. This Frankie is charming and winsome. People like this Frankie, and who wouldn't? If you first met Frankie, this is probably the guy you would encounter. You might spend thirty minutes or a couple of hours with him, then read this book and conclude that I'm crazy for writing a load a shit.

The fourth personality is the guy who will try and kill me. This Frankie is neither verbal nor friendly. This is who he is when he needs to handle shit. Whenever he's wronged or feels like he needs to send a message, this is the guy who does the dirty work. Trust me; I've met this one far too many times.

Once you know Frankie as well as me, you will observe how he can spin into another personality as quickly as a greased pig at the fair. One minute you think you have him figured out and what he wants, the next minute it's an entirely different person. The switch can take place smack in the middle of a conversation. When you observe him, you can see a physical change that takes place. His eyes change color. They are naturally hazel, but when he assumes another personality, they turn black.

When he described to the shrinks about the time he was strangling me, he told them he was watching the entire event from up above. While he was choking me, with his hands around my neck, he was looking down from up above somewhere and swears he couldn't do anything to stop himself. It was some type of out-of-body experience. That being said, the entity that the medium spoke of, and his out of body seem to me as the same thing. Some might even call that a possession. Before our marriage ended, we were going to three psychiatrists, and I learned they were talking to one another about this. Back when he had been in the room locked up, he had threatened suicide again one day while my daughter was present. The shrink called and asked if he had been called into work that day, and I said no then began to tell her what's going on. She said he called to lie to her about cancelling the appointment. She said it was her duty to call the police for suicide, so she did. He was brought back awhile later after police found him headed to Vegas with three thousand dollars to go party! He nicknamed the shrink "man hater" and refused to ever see her again. When he lied to the shrinks, they put him into a "no-no" file. This meant he did not want treatment and was lying to them. Upon three times, they would refuse him from then on for the entire state. I told my shrink, things were not right with the other shrink who was doing the marriage stuff. She is the one I had known for several years, that Frankie was playing games with one of the other shrinks. Frankie had told me he had years of experience bullshitting shrinks. Frankie had said some things about me that weren't true like I'm an alcoholic and the crazy one. When I arrived at our appointment, the doctor was all over me. I told him that he didn't know what he was dealing with when it comes to Frankie.

I had the divorce papers completed, but they were on hold. About a week prior to filing them, I had not told a soul about my plans. I had to be secretive because I knew Frankie would go crazy. When he was out of control, I knew I might be in danger for my life. I had a plan in place that would keep me safe once the papers were submitted.

The plan was to enter a rehab facility for 30 days, so no one would know my location. At the same time, I filed for a restraining order to keep Frankie away, which was my safest bet. Otherwise, I would worry about my dad's safety as well as mine. I had tied up loose ends at work. After spending two weeks in prayer, I was confident God said, "Go for it."

I knew it was time. It had been a long time coming. Although everyone knew I was going into rehab, they did not know about the divorce happening at the same time. I actually felt safe about the process.

My only worry was Dad who was living in the house at the time. He was in ill health with a busted hip and needed a caretaker. I had booted Frankie out of the house a few days before getting Dad home from the rest home. Although I allowed him back for five days, I kicked him out again. He had called and said he was lonely. One night at dinner we argued about him putting our affairs on Catherine again. He yelled at me in the restaurant to "shut the fuck up". The night I kicked him out again, I had come home to have him yell at me for no reason and him saying that I deserved it. I gave him his suitcase and told him not to call and say he was lonely. I then took him to the door and told him not to let it hit him on the way out. In between those times, Frankie had broken into my home on a few occasions, put a gun in one of his dresser drawers, and slashed my tire which went out at 75 miles an hour on the expressway in the fast lane. My sister flew in to stay at the house and tend to Dad.

Apparently, Frankie was also planning something that same weekend since I was leaving for rehab. My cousin, the one Frankie was sweet on in Vegas, was flying in, and my son and his wife were coming in from Missouri. When I learned of all these plans, I was grateful that I already had a temporary restraining order.

When my sister arrived, I told her she was just there to take care of Dad until I got out of rehab. When she arrived, I told her about the divorce and what I was planning. I specifically instructed her not to allow Frankie into the house or to get near to Dad.

Do you remember the old saying, "The best laid plans of mice and men often go awry?" That's precisely what happened. Things didn't go well. I think what Frankie was planning once I checked into rehab was to give my Dad to David, or my sister to care for, to take back to Missouri. He would then take the house and file for divorce himself.

I had been in rehab for four days when I was asked to speak with the Director. It seems my insurance was refusing to pay for the treatment since I had not been diagnosed as an alcoholic. This was my third time going, and third time told I am not an alcoholic. In fact, I hadn't even had a drink for weeks when I checked in. They were scrambling to find a way to cover the costs and suggested I accept some type of psychological disorder.

A few hours after that conversation, my appendix burst. I had been feeling ill all day, but they wouldn't let me call an ambulance or take me in. They didn't allow anyone to leave rehab once they check in. Finally, that evening, I threatened the night girl and demanded that someone needed to get me the fuck out of this place. She allowed me to call my sister who came and took me to the hospital. I stayed there for seven days.

Although I had warned my sister not to let Frankie in the house, she did. However, I never did find out if my cousin and Frankie got together, she would only lie to me.

During my hospital stay, which extended to two hospitals, and a week to get my appendix removed, I had no control over what was happening at the house. However, as soon as I was released from the hospital, I took a cab to the house, and my sister quickly took off and left town. She obviously didn't want to see me. She had dinner with Frankie a couple of times while I was gone and even allowed him to come to the house and to be around Dad. I heard her talking to my mom on the phone as my mom began to yell "get the fuck out of there". As she left, she looked over to Dad and said, "I'm going now; are you sure you don't want to come?"

He replied, "No, I'm going to stay here." I learned the next week, my dad's account number had been changed to the Missouri address along with his new debit card going there and his social security check of direct deposit. Of course, when I asked him about it, he couldn't remember. They had taken advantage of his memory not being too good, and he couldn't remember.

The saddest part of this whole thing is that my father, 80 years old and recovering from a broken hip, was just learning to walk again and his mind was not all there. He had been on dialysis for a decade and had to give up his drivers' license after getting lost a few times. The assholes in my life—Frankie, my sister, my mom, and my son—were trying to take advantage of an old man for his Social Security check. They wanted to get him to Missouri where they were staying as part of their plan to make sure I was homeless, penniless, and destitute.

After coming home from the hospital and the surgery, I was still weak and dealing with my own medical procedures. Dad was in no shape to help with anything. He was on dialysis, and the center where he received treatment was only blocks from our house, so I was able to get him there even though I was not supposed to drive. My first court date for the purpose of enforcing the restraining order was postponed because

I was in no condition to make it downtown to the courthouse. I still needed a second surgery as well.

When the date finally came, I was shocked when my attorney didn't even show up. He sent an associate without informing me. This associate was young and unprepared, so I was hung out to dry. Catherine, my daughter, showed up to testify against me. My son and his wife testified for Frankie via the phone. I found out that I was being watched and they brought up that I cancelled the original date because I couldn't drive and that they knew of me driving Dad to dialysis during that period. Consequently, I couldn't get a restraining order and he's had free reign ever since. On two occasions, he would just show up after cutting the lock on the gate with bolt cutters. One visit, he asked for a copy of our marriage certificate to use to add me to his new insurance after I had already asked for Cobra insurance. When I returned with the copy outside, I said, "aren't you going to ask how I'm doing since my first surgery?" He exploded and said, "That's what I hate about you." I turned, walked in the house and locked the door. He came up trying to open it, then the side door, looking crazy with the black eyes. I told him to leave as I was calling the cops. He left. During the time our divorce was in process of being finalized, the police were called out several times. On some occasions, multiple times in one day. The week prior to his move out date, scheduled by the court documents, the police were at my home four times. They decided to investigate him wondering why he was not afraid of the police and chose to keep returning after being told to leave. The first officer asked me if he was a "psycho". I said yes. The police told me that Frankie was paying the neighbors to keep an eye on me and report whatever they observed at both properties. They asked that I get a restraining order. I explained of not being able to get one, and they said I should find somewhere to go then. They really couldn't be of much help. Move out day for Frankie, I had it written in the court documents after that day, to not allow him to come. He was the first one there, of course, and brought 12 skinheads to hurt my boyfriend. "Send out bruiser", he yelled. Police were there all day.

After the failed attempt to get the restraining order, Frankie and the judge had a conversation. I learned that he had applied for a job in another city and I knew nothing about it. He was rushing to get away. He had already drained my bank accounts with the help of David, my son. The reason the kids were helping their Dad is that they were holding on to the hope of continuing to receive his money. When he talked to the judge about moving away, the judge was pissed off that he even tried to cash out his retirement to keep it from me. Even after the judge told him he was not allowed to access those funds, he tried to do it several times. He stole my mail, changed my mailing address twice, refused to pay me alimony. When he filed again, he had twelve counts of contempt of court for not paying me. I should've put him in jail for a long time, but I took my attorney's advice to take his retirement. He even tried to do his refinance to remove my name without paying the year owed for alimony! My attorney was sure to get me a check. I watched him and his attorney sit there and lie on every occasion even while under oath. I heard my kids lie to the court under oath too. My second lawyer said, "Frankie gets off on pissing you off, he thinks it's fun!"

The two and a half years it took for the divorce to be finalized, once and for all, was filled with anger, violence, and foolishness—precisely what I expected. It's not unusual for a divorce to be contentious, but a divorce involving a guy like Frankie gives new meaning to difficult. My third attorney I hired, after my second one made a deal with Frankie in his office and I fired him for it, told me that this was one of the worst cases she had ever seen and she had been doing divorces for 16 years. Every step of the way was painful because his primary goal was to make me suffer. He was so committed to screwing me financially that he quit the best job he ever had in order to move out of state in an attempt to avoid paying alimony. I knew it was planned when I overheard his lawyer in court discuss his returning to eliminate alimony. He did file to do that almost a year later, and had failed to pay me one cent during that whole time.

The police were frequent visitors to my house. They would chase him off, and he would come right back. They asked why Frankie was not even afraid of the cops. Unless you understand his dysfunction, it's impossible to comprehend his actions. He broke into my house a couple of times, sometimes to retrieve something and other times just to scare me.

I made it through the divorce, and I'm still alive, a claim that I was not always sure I'd be alive. My second lawyer, who liked him, had made a deal with him in his office to get me to give him some additional things. That's why I fired him! Now that I understand this stuff a little bit better, in his mind it's just fun to hurt people. It's always a game, and always about him.

# CONCLUSION

Whenever you tell a story, there's hope for a good ending. Something like, "They all lived happily ever after." I wish I could end my story with those words, or with something even remotely similar. Alas, I can't. There is no happy ending to my saga. Yet … But, telling this has been a beneficial, cathartic experience for me.

Frankie and I were divorced. The legal process took almost three years, only because he continued to fight and refuse to follow court orders. We went our separate ways, but it was anything but a clean break. Obviously, we had the question of two children who we shared. Even though they were adults by the time we divorced, as a parent you want to continue the relationship with your child. In the best-case scenario, you hope to become good friends and share your life together for the remainder of your days.

That has not been the case. It has been over four years without any contact with my daughter. My son did text a few times, but left me with the fact that neither of them wants anything to do with me ever again. He refused to let me come by their home to drop of my dad's belongings after he died, and before I moved again. As far as I know, they are still in communication with their father, and as long as that's the case, I don't expect they'll have much to do with me. Frankie had threatened me as the final legal proceedings were winding down, that I will "never have a relationship with my kids or my grandkids". I'm convinced my kids will not come around me until their father goes after them, and he will someday. It will be my son first as he is still living in the home his father owns. They are both just like him in many ways, especially their love of money. Right now, Frankie is their source of money, so I'm out of the loop. One thing that's truly ironic is that David wants to be a psychiatrist. I had learned at my first court appearance David was fired from his job for hitting a man who was trying to steal a doughnut. Reminded me of his father.

I don't have any interaction with Frankie any longer, a fact that I'm pleased about.

He started to be very nice as legal issues were finished and he asked about being friends, but I shut that down after a brief text remembering all of his threats and lies. Somehow, he always seems to find where I'm living. When I moved the first time, he had my old neighbor call with a lie to get my address. I gave her my sister's address only to receive a card from him three days later to my correct address. I guess I was being stalked again, then new court filings. So, now I have moved again. To be honest, it wouldn't be a surprise if he showed up someday and did me serious harm. However, I try not to live in fear of that happening.

All our legal connections have been finalized, so there's no reason we need to have contact. It would be great if we could all get together like a healthy family and celebrate events and enjoy grandchildren, but since my kids are not interested, that doesn't happen either. As long as they believe that Frankie will be the great financial provider, they're not going to have anything to do with me. They don't want to run the risk of being cut off.

Frankie makes a lot of money, which is extremely important to him. His job is to make drinkable water from poo. Yes, I do mean he turns sewage into drinkable water. His job provides a sizable salary. While we were married, he worked for the city, and they paid for his education to learn how to do this type of work. Who knew it would become such a valuable skill.

The happy ending to my story was the finalization of our divorce. It was a huge relief to be out from under the shit I had endured for 30 years. In case you're wondering why I wrote the book, I'll admit it is not an uplifting story, nor is it a tale of overcoming adversity and accomplishing something worthwhile. The reason is that several psychologists who worked with Frankie and me suggested I tell the story from my perspective. Frequently, when we talked about Frankie, and as they pumped me for information to help them understand him, they encouraged me to write a book.

When working with shrinks, I would tell them "This is how I bust him in a lie, or this is how you get him to snap."

These were techniques that can only be learned by living with an individual. The psychologists knew that I had a great deal more information that would be of value, not only as they worked with Frankie, but also as they dealt with others having similar issues.

Mental illness has always existed in both of his families. It all came together when Frankie and I got together, kind of like a perfect storm. Consequently, I worry often about my kids. Not only was the family DNA passed on to them, but also, they witnessed an enormous amount of destructive behavior as well as Frankie and me continually fighting, often violently. The vicious cycle has to stop somewhere. Since some of it might be genetic, I told my son to pay careful attention because the apple doesn't fall far from the tree.

Another motivation is my spiritual journey. I indicated earlier that the spiritual life has always been important to me. It's why I became a born-again Christian and why I continue on my current spiritual path.

Even though we live with our hopes for the future, we learn by looking back to the past. I think about that time after David was born and Frankie's mother began telling me stories about how he was and the similarities in them. I now understand why she moved away when he graduated, it was her way of getting out of what she had come to realize was a hopeless relationship. She saw it as her way of getting away from him. At the time, I thought it was awful. However, after my son was old enough to make it on his own, I scrambled hard to get him out of the house and away from his father. Just as I had done with Catherine, my daughter. I worked hard to get David and his girlfriend into our house in Missouri, so they had a chance to make it on their own. I knew he was just like his father and if I kept him near it would end in tragedy.

There are certain people or personality types you just need to walk away from as fast as possible. They just don't care about anyone else, and they thrive off people who will help them. Like my dad always told me, they will never change. The shrink said, "they don't think there's anything wrong with them". I firmly believe you can't help people that don't want help!

Now that I've related my story, I want to provide some meaning to the various episodes of my life described in the preceding pages. I begin by explaining why Frankie was continually diagnosed as a sociopath. First, a definition.

The first chapter began with a definition of a sociopath as a person with a personality disorder manifesting itself in extreme antisocial attitudes and behavior, a lack of empathy, and a lack of conscience. To have a personality disorder simply means that you have an unhealthy and often rigid way of dealing with situations and people. The person with the disorder probably doesn't even recognize they have a problem because it seems perfectly natural to them. Typically, a personality disorder does not manifest itself until the teenage years, and for the fortunate ones, it can lessen as they advance into middle age and beyond.

Frankie's problems did come early, perhaps even as a child, but it was during his teens that it was first recognized as a severe continuing issue. The bad news is that he has not improved from aging. In fact, most psychologists would say there are no studies that indicate a sociopath can change. Treatment is challenging, and the massive burden falls on those who love them and live with them. Some experts have resigned themselves to the fact that treatment is not possible and the best thing for the non-sociopath is to get away from them entirely.

Research has shown that the typical treatments for bad behavior do not affect sociopaths. That explains why he's not afraid of the police. I concur with that conclusion because I tried them all on Frankie. It has been determined that punishment, even sending them to prison does not work. In spite of all his drug dealing, Frankie never went to prison. I'm sure if he ever did, it wouldn't take him long to manipulate the system to his advantage. I tried punishment numerous times. I don't remember how many times I threw him out of the house, but I always let him come back, I usually apologized, and we went on as if nothing happened. As I have said, allowing this treatment and for him to stay was my fault too.

The logical solution is therapy and counseling. However, many studies have shown that such an approach is useless with sociopaths. Once again, I sent Frankie to numerous shrinks, and they tried for years to no avail. Successful therapy requires the desire to change, and Frankie never wanted to change. He even told me, when I first had him begin the process to seek help, was when he wanted to leave and get divorced. It was nothing more than a game to him.

And our relationship was nothing more than a game also, as well as a lie.

Another approach is medication, but I don't need to remind you that we tried that extensively. The reason medication doesn't work is because he doesn't have an illness; he has a personality disorder. Or multiple disorders would be more correct. It's not caused by a virus or germ that can be cured.

An approach often tried by those who live with sociopaths is to threaten and beg. However, you soon learn that it's nothing more than a game to them, a way of beating the system. If they can get away with something then they win; if they get caught and suffer punishment, who cares? Frankie never cared when I threatened to leave or take something from him. Remember, he doesn't have feelings for another person, so threats have no power. The final text I received from him after asking why all the hate, he replied, "that would assume I have feelings for you, and I don't.". This is all good information to know after a 30 year relationship with someone.

The problems between Frankie and I were intensified because I'm an empath, and intuitive, and I have a deep sense of what's going on with other people. I care deeply about others, and Frankie cares for no one but himself. Trying to teach a sociopath how to feel emotion is like trying to teach a refrigerator how to fly. His brain isn't wired to feel empathy or even normal emotions. I witnessed this with friends, deaths, and animals. And, he just doesn't care.

Let me take this a step further and explain that Frankie is not only a sociopath; he's a narcissistic sociopath. Not only does he lack empathy toward others, but he also has a tremendous concern for his own needs. He is convinced that he deserves to exploit others for what he can get out of them and then cast them aside when he's finished. A friend joked one day and said. "Get over the no father thing. The world doesn't owe you." Our friend the attorney once said, "I have never met a human being with as big of an ego as Frankie." Two days after I filed divorce he's dating my cousin. Within weeks, he moved another woman in with him to live. Fear of being alone with the "voices" in his head maybe. I assume he has gone back to pleasing himself, his needs, and his "cocktail".

When it came to relating to other people, he was cold, calculating, and manipulative. His only concern for others is how they can benefit him.

One of the characteristics of a narcissistic sociopath is they never feel guilt or

BRUISED BUT NOT BROKEN

remorse. Consequently, they never apologize. That always drove me crazy with Frankie. The few times he did offer an apology it was evident that he was doing it in order to get something from you. In other words, he would say he was sorry for striking me because he knew it was the only way I would ever let him back in the house. He was never sorry.

That trait also helps to understand his constant lying. Even when you catch him red-handed in a lie, he will never admit to it. Sometimes when caught he will become very angry and violent. Just as he does if you tell him NO to something. He continually asserts that he's not lying, does his spin on the reality of things and you give up. You can't reason with him or provide evidence because he won't accept it because, in his mind, it's not a lie.

Another concept I discovered while trying to understand Frankie was "gaslighting." The term originated with a 1938 stage play that was adapted into a film in the early 1940's starring Ingrid Bergman. The original story is about a man who murdered a woman in the upstairs apartment. He would go up at night to look for the jewels she had hidden. When he turned on the gaslight to aid in his search, the gaslights downstairs would always dim. When his wife noticed the gaslights were dimming, she approached her husband, and he finally convinced her she was crazy. He would hide things from her then blame her for loosing things or not remembering where she put them. The term "gaslighting" came to mean a deliberate attempt to change another person's perception of reality. I call it a spin on the reality of what's really going on. Some could call it brainwashing.

Several people told me during the time I was with Frankie that I was being "gaslighted." It's a form of mental abuse used by people seeking power. Frankie would gaslight me to cover up all his secret behaviors. That's why he consistently lied about what he did, even when I knew the truth. He was striving to change my perception. Most authorities say that gaslighting is typically used by a person who is a narcissist, addict, or sociopath. Bingo! Frankie hit the trifecta.

A typical tool is to destroy the self-esteem of another person. One of the most frequent ways Frankie did that to me was when it came to sex. He was always talking about how I was a bitch, or how he hated the way I looked. In response, I was willing to try whatever kinky suggestion he made, except changing or adding partners, or I would dress like a whore if that's what he wanted. Those things were uncomfortable for me, but I was manipulated into doing them just to please him. I had sexual needs and hoped acquiescing to his wishes would attract him to me. It didn't!

Frankie's addictions were legendary. His attachment to drugs, and porn, then graduating to hookers or the cheating impacted every area of our lives and time together. The majority of our fights were initiated by these issues by me. He was controlled by them. His mind was so warped by these objects that it was impossible to reason with him. He once told me that the reason he was so attracted to porn was because the women didn't expect anything from him. They gave him pleasure, but he didn't have to do anything for them. He even told me one time that those women liked him. That's

61

insane. They weren't women—they were only photographs and movies. They had no idea he even existed, and could not give him anything in reality.

Once he received the inheritance, Frankie had a new addiction—money. He always loved spending money, but once he had it to spend it fiercely gripped his life. I think he was attracted to it because he realized it gave him power over other people. People would bow to his every wish once they realized he had money. He thought I did too, but I always told him I loved him.

Another diagnosis that Frankie received over the years was PTSD. We hear a great deal about that condition today and we typically think it terms of war or some kind of serious accident. However, many people suffer from PTSD because of childhood sexual assault. Most people return to normal over time. However, there are some who actually get worse over time. When that happens, they find it difficult to be in touch with their feelings and emotions, preferring to isolate themselves from those who care about them. In addition, they may demonstrate outbursts of anger.

All these symptoms describe both Frankie, and some, my mother. In fact, just recently, Mom confided that she had been sexually abused as a child by a relative. I'm continually amazed at how much alike these two crucial people are in my life. Especially the completed childhood dramas are almost identical.

My story will not be complete unless it includes my own drunken rants. I can go into an unbelievable rage when I've been drinking. It will make your skin crawl. Many of our fights began or were escalated because of my drinking. I've never pretended that I was innocent concerning the problems in our relationship. I always thought, the drunk guy lives through the accident, right?

I'm a highly sensitive empath. Not only am I highly sensitive myself, but I also pick up emotions and feelings from others as well. I'm living with a sociopath. What do you pick up from someone without emotions? Most of what I felt from him was anger, rage, and hate. He has no feelings for others and doesn't give a fuck about anyone but himself. We were exact polar opposites in a relationship.

Also, I have always used humor to protect myself. Most of the time I consider the source, as my mom and grandma used to say, and think, "This is hilarious." Mental illness can be funny as well as traumatic. Sometimes I would wonder what planet was this guy living on? My humor is a resource for coping. Rather than leaving him, I coped by laughing at him.

Everybody asks, I mean Everyone, "How in the hell did you stay there so long?"

That's the most frequent question I am asked. Looking back now, it's clear that it was a mistake, but that conclusion was not so clear at the time. Through counseling, I discovered that I had trouble with "stuffing" my emotions. That's what they call it when don't deal with your feelings. It means that you just tuck them away. The problem is that the emotions don't disappear. They're still there, waiting to come out some day.

One of the most significant stuffed emotions was anger. It typically centered around something like this—Really, you fucked a hooker, and you come home and tell me what?"

Counselors told me I had to get it out. I needed to speak up. That's probably why I drank. I would get so hammered at night and just lay into him, not physically but verbally, hoping he would feel like the smallest tick on a cat's ass. I started doing this all the time.

He tried to kill me four times. It never hurt him because he doesn't give a shit. It's really not in me to hurt people anyways unless I'm attacked first. Then I will fight, but I don't care to as I believe things can be handled with words. He couldn't care less what I think about him. All he cares about is what he wants. The probable reason he stayed with me was because I made shit work. I handled things. He's like a child. He does what he wants to do when he wants to do them. He was not concerned about bills, responsibility, money, and I handled it all so he didn't have to. He has no clue about money. I handled the kids, my dad, the home, worked, and took care of all the finances. He was free to surf, do drugs, deal, work, and on occasion spend time with family.

I think he stayed because he needed me for some of the things a spouse would do but not for emotional support or sex. I felt like his "party buddy" most of time sitting there with all his other ones. With his porn and after he had the vasectomy which eliminated the possibility of having children, he didn't seem to want me for sex any longer. I always considered him a third child. In fact, in many ways, I had to take care of him just like he was a young child. Growing up, he never learned how to act because he didn't have parents around to teach him anything. Last I knew, he had married a woman who is 16 years older than him, so essentially when he left me, he finally found a Mama who would look after him.

I wanted an equal partner, someone to help with the family stuff, raise the kids, and provide my emotional needs. I kept telling him I didn't want another kid, but that's what he needed. Perhaps the reason Frankie stayed with me is his fear of being alone. Sometimes he would leave for a few days, and I think he was trying to see if he could live alone. He would occasionally talk about being suicidal, but I'm not sure if he was. He said when he was alone, the voices in his head were very bad. They told him to do things, and he called it "the dark place". My mother was the same way, deathly afraid of being alone, but now seems to enjoy it, she says. Frankie told me once that he had a fear of abandonment, perhaps because his parents virtually abandoned him. He always had to have the radio on, a constant noise early in the marriage. He said if it was quiet he heard voices in his head.

During the time we ran the shop, right after he got all the money, we were both changing in a variety of ways. We had some phenomenal fights. One, in particular, happened because I hired my own shrink to help me understand how to do business with this guy. I mentioned to her about Frankie's suicide threats. It wasn't anything new, but I wanted professional advice on how to handle them. She asked a bunch of questions about the availability of drugs or weapons and if he had ever made any actual attempts. She suggested if it came up again that I should try him, see if he really wants to do it or if he's just talking smack.

One day I received a call, and I was a long distance from the shop. It was Frankie, and he was at the shop. He threatened to kill himself. I picked up the pace to get back to him, and when I arrived, he was locked in the bathroom. I tried to talk him out of the bathroom. I looked around the shop and realized that if you want to kill yourself, there are plenty of tools that will do the job lying around. About a half an hour later he came out, and there was nothing in the bathroom. He didn't even have any pills. He sat down and stared at the computer.

When I didn't see anything, I said, "Look, are you actually going to kill yourself or not? I've got better things to do," and then I walked out.

Years later when I brought up the subject of his suicide threats to one of the shrinks, Frankie admitted, "I just do that for attention."

After the episode at the shop, he never called me with a threat again. Occasionally, he would tell me that he had tried to do something after the fact, but I never believed him.

On one occasion, Frankie threatened suicide with my daughter there. According to the law, the shrink was obligated to report it to the police. Consequently, the police went looking for him and found in heading out of town to Vegas with thousands of dollars in his pocket. This was a real problem in Frankie's mind because now there was an official file on him.

That kind of shit happens all the time when you're dealing with an unstable person. One day while Frankie was living in his "locked room," my Dad came to me and said, "I've got my suitcase packed. Let's go to Missouri and never come back."

He was angry and not usually like that, but he added, "Let's just get the fuck out and leave crazy here."

I told him that I couldn't. Our daughter had just moved back in and I didn't want to leave her alone with him. At the time, I had a key to Nick's place and a bug out bag for when things got heated and I felt threatened. Catherine knew about this as I told her not to worry when she saw me leaving. I asked her if she was afraid of him and she assured me she wasn't, and she was an adult, old enough to make her own decisions, but I just couldn't leave her alone. At one point he said he had become born again Christian. I had a pastor come to help with marriage stuff thinking that might work. After his second visit, he quit coming. Frankie said he didn't like that he admitted liking women. The pastor told me on the phone, Frankie refused to take any responsibility for anything that was going on. I'm sure Frankie lied again.

I was constantly encouraged to have Frankie arrested and locked up. The attorney, and my shrink, told me they would be able to do a full evaluation on him and perhaps get him help. But I realized if I did they would probably only hold him for 72 hours and then what happens to me?

I'm aware that I haven't answered the question yet of why I stayed. I think the answer is simply that I loved Frankie. Perhaps it's because of the deep empathy I felt for him from the beginning. I wanted to help him, and I firmly believe that I did everything I knew to do to help him. My friends in the spiritual community tell me that my relationship with Frankie did considerable damage to me physically, psychologically, and emotionally. I don't disagree with that assessment. It's 30 years of my life that I could have used in a much more productive manner.

Although I've been through a lot, I'm not looking for pity. I made my choice, and I'm willing to live with the consequences. I'm moving on and rebuilding my life. I have hopes and plans for the future, and I'm living with my eyes forward.

My father told me about the community in Minnesota where he grew up. He described a lonely asylum that sat at the foot of a hill on the outskirts of town. It was a large, multi-storied building where they put people with serious mental disorders—things like schizophrenia and bipolar disorder (used to be called manic depressant). If you go back into the not too distant past of these places, you will find they were called lunatic asylums. It's the kind of place where a guy like Frankie would be confined.

I don't pretend to know the right thing to do, but it would have been nice if Frankie could have been helped decades ago. My life, my children, my father, and numerous others would have lived far different lives without the overbearing presence of a selfish, sociopath influencing every aspect of our existence.

When we first moved in together, Frankie reached out and gave me a big, loving bear hug. He said, "I want you to let the walls down."

The words were comforting. I had spent many years building up protection from all the people and experiences that tried to harm me. Hopefully it was time to let it all go and relax and enjoy life, so I listened to his words, and I let down the walls.

I should have left them up. As soon as they were down, Frankie changed my life and left a swath of destruction that will be with me for a long time. Over time, whatever has happened, I know there are good people out there. And I survived.

As you read my story, I might not sound as broken as one would expect, but the truth is that I have been shattered numerous times. My heart of glass in a billion pieces, put back together, then busted again over and over. Tears have flowed down my cheeks until my tear ducts were dry. Like my grandma said, "Honey I've cried a river of tears." I have fought through depression, anxiety, panic attacks, wrestled with hate and anger, vented my rage on living and inanimate objects just to still be alive. I had my second surgery while going through the divorce that was screwed up, and led me through another 4 surgeries in one week! And I survived that as well. I'm able to rebuild through faith in the good that life has to offer, and that's the only reason I'm still here.

# POSTSCRIPT

This is the postscript to my story:

Recently I heard an interview with Christine Northrop, M.D. titled "Dodging Energy Vampires". She defined the term as Personality Disorders including sociopath, narcissist, borderline personality disorder, psychopath, or other personality disorders. She discussed researchers have proven over the last 10 years with pet scans and MRI's these people are born with this, and these disorders are NOT caused by childhood issues. They will Never change their characteristics and that psychology does NOT work on them. She said they are waiting for the mental health community to "Get a grip on them", and "Their tactics have been overlooked by the mental health community for decades because they are so good at their tactics and behaviors". She added they are totally unconscious, have a disregard for what's right or wrong, lack of remorse, predators that hook you with sob stories, and pathological liars.

One of my last appointments with my shrink I had read a great article in one of their psychology magazines. In this article it was discussing how charming, charismatic, and attractive these personality disorders can be which helps them attract people easily. Due to this tactic they are multiplying, and the article believes the next century to be filled completely with people with personality disorders. The article was scary to me but really seemed to make perfect sense.

Frankie – I really don't know what's going on with Frankie since our divorce was final. In our last few text messages, I was told he was remarried, but I've learned not to believe much of what he says. I did see an older girlfriend at one of the court dates, but I'm not sure if they're still together. In threatening terms, I was told I would never have a relationship with my kids or grandkids. I understood it as a threat and I'm confident he will use them and manipulate them, until the day I die. I'm still wondering if I may be a grandma now because of the threat about grandchildren. My children are the only thing remaining that he can use to hurt me.

My kids, Catherine and David – I have not had any contact with them for a long time. As far as I know they are close to their father, close with each other, and both share some of the same dysfunctional qualities. I've been told they want nothing to do with me.

Dad - He passed away in July 2016. During his final days, I spent as much time with him as possible, helping him with the transition. He had made a decision to die, it just took his body a couple of years to fulfill his wish. After him living with me his whole life, and helping to raise my kids, I know his heart was broken before he passed away from them disowning him as well as me. I'm so blessed and grateful to have spent so many wonderful years with my father. I released his ashes in Sep. 2016 in the ocean with my sister, and friend in attendance. Mom refused to come.

Mom – Shortly after I filed for divorce with Frankie, Mom's husband died in an accident. Mom was able to spend some time with Dad before he died and she also was able to be with her baby brother before he died in 2017. She has her own place and we communicate weekly. Her health is not very good, and she does not communicate with family anymore except for my sister and I. She says she is enjoying living alone, which she has never done before and was a bit fearful. Her personality is basically the same as it was 40 years ago.

Sister - Diane is well and living near Mom. We've become closer dealing with issues concerning our parents. She's been loving and helpful in my life. I love her and am grateful she's here.

I've moved on the best I know how. After 30 years of caring for everyone, I lost my entire family in a brief amount of time. I'm rebuilding my life and hoping to get settled. I've moved twice since the divorce and meeting new people. I've been traveling, starting a new business, and I received my Reiki Master Certification. I have great hopes for my future! Especially for this book!

My greatest hope for this book is for it to help someone! If I may be able to just reach one person to help, it will all be worth it for me. Namaste

Printed in the United States
By Bookmasters